MW00619575

STARING
AT THE CROSSHAIRS

by Derrick D. Bartlett

TO CRAIG,

TRAIN HARD, FIGHT EASY.

Derrick

WIISAD
B O O K S
A DIVISION OF SNIPERCRAFT, INC.

Also by Derrick D. Bartlett
Snipercraft: The Art of the Police Sniper, 1999

Staring at the Crosshairs
by Derrick D. Bartlett

Copyright ©2004 by WIISAD Books

ISBN 0-9748969-0-X
Printed in the United States of America

Published by WIISAD Books, a division of Snipercraft, Inc.

Direct inquiries and/or orders to WIISAD Books,
472 Lakeside Circle, Fort Lauderdale, FL 33326-4103
wiisadbooks@aol.com • (954) 389-0829

Dedication

This book is dedicated to the men
and women who are doing the job.
It is for every sniper who has chosen to answer the page,
pick up the rifle, and shoulder the responsibility.
Succeed, because there is no allowance for failure.

To the Kristina's of the world, and the men and women
sworn to protect them.

"We sleep safe in our beds because rough men
stand ready to visit violence on those who would do us harm."

—George Orwell—

I don't know the origin of this passage, but the message is priceless. This has no direct link to sniping, but when I read it, I felt it was a sentiment worth passing on to other tactical operators. Heed the warning.

I am more powerful than the combined armies of the world. I have destroyed more men than all the wars of all the nations. I massacre thousands of people every year.

I am more deadly than bullets, and I have wrecked more homes than the mightiest guns. I find my victims among the rich and poor alike, the young and old, the strong and weak. Widows know me to their everlasting sorrow.

I loom up in such proportions that I cast my shadow over every field of labor. I lurk in unseen places and do most of my work silently. You are warned against me, yet you heed me not. I am relentless, merciless, and cruel.

I am everywhere.

I bring sickness, degradation and death, yet few seek me out to destroy me. I will give you nothing and take all that you have. I am your worst enemy. I am Carelessness.

Unknown

Author's Note—

I don't want anyone reading this book to feel as if I am being exclusionary by the use of certain terminology. The use of masculine pronouns in referring to snipers does not ignore the presence and contributions of female snipers currently working in the tactical field. Using the all-inclusive "he or she" gets irritating after awhile.

Likewise, I don't want military snipers to feel left out of this audience. Admittedly, I have never been a military sniper, and my personal knowledge of their training and mission is limited. This book is geared toward police snipers, because that is what I know. However, with the changes in the theaters in which military snipers are being deployed, hopefully some of what is talked about here will appeal to them as well.

Derrick Bartlett has made possibly the single greatest contribution to sniping that could have been made; he started us talking. In addition to being an accomplished sniper himself, he has served as a teacher, author, and leader. He cares deeply about sniping, and snipers.

Our job is to save lives. By encouraging snipers to share information, and prepare ourselves for what may come, he has helped save careers, families, and lives. He is also an honorable man, and a good friend to snipers everywhere. Now he has raised the bar again...

Russ Clagett
United States Army

The law enforcement sniper has never had a more trusted friend and tireless mentor than Derrick Bartlett.

Brian K. Sain, Detective
Port Arthur, TX Police Dept.

In the world of Police sniping, no one does it better and is more knowledgeable than Derrick. I have attended many training classes over the years and I have found no one as passionate to this art. He is truly the go-to guy when it comes to training, and if you are ever involved in a sniper-related shooting, he is the person you want on your defense team. I am proud and honored to call him my friend and comrade in arms.

Chris Savard
Orlando, FL Police Dept.

Derrick's contributions prove how one person can make a difference. He has made a difference, and, perhaps more importantly, he has instilled in others the desire to make a difference. He is passionate about training, and it shows in his teaching, and through his guidance. Today, snipers are a stronger community because of people like Derrick Bartlett. Derrick has put the word "sniper" back in our job description, and we can be proud. "Be ready, don't get ready." Having known Derrick as a friend, as well as a colleague, I can say without reservation that he truly lives up to the honorable title of "sniper."

Richard Morey
Coordinator, Law Enforcement Programs
SFCC Criminal Justice Academy

Derrick has gained the utmost respect from the sniper community. He has gained this respect by his extensive knowledge and dedication to the art of sniping.

Derrick has single-handedly developed a network for sharing critical knowledge and experiences that must be shared in order to make us all more professional snipers. He is our hub of information. A man that believes it is not what we do, but who we are, snipers.

Lt. Paul J. Renkas
Waukesha County, WI Sheriffs Dept.

Contents

Appendix

PROLOGUE

The Shot Not Taken

He was lying in a hammock, beachside on some island. The ocean breeze was soothing, taking the edge off the sun speckling his face through the trees. The day would have been perfect except for that insistent buzzing sound in the background. He wasn't quit sure where it was coming from, but the sniper wished it would go away. Whoever was nudging him, trying to rouse him from his reverie, was also starting to annoy him.

"Honey, wake up. Your pager is going off." The voice in the distance was much closer now. So was the intermittent buzzing sound. The beach faded away as his eyes slit open to see a ceiling fan above his head. He remembered where he was and recognized the hum of his pager vibrating on the headboard above him. He retrieved it and after reading the display forced himself upright. He half-turned to his wife and softly said, "Callout." He stood up, grabbed his gear bag from the closet and headed out of the room. As always, his wife told him to be careful as he closed the bedroom door.

With practiced ease, the sniper dressed and gathered his equipment. Within minutes of awakening to the page, he was headed out the door. The humid night air helped to chase the cobwebs that remained. He double checked the information on his pager display and fixed his destination in his mind. As he started toward the city, he turned on his radio and advised the SWAT dispatcher he was enroute.

The scene was the usual hive of activity. Flashing strobes lit up the night and outlined the target area. The sniper parked in the secured area and sought out his team leader.

"We have an armed barricade. The guy who lives in the rear apartment was seen standing outside, shooting a shotgun into the air. When patrol showed up, he went in and refused to come out. They reported hearing him racking the shotgun and decided to back off and call us. Right now, he's refusing to answer the phone. Set up on him, and we'll go from there." The briefing was short and sweet. The team leader pointed out the building, gave the sniper team a look at a hasty sketch made by a patrol officer.

The sniper and his partner, Surfer, gathered their gear and left the command post. Their target location was an L-shaped, single story apartment building. The subject was holed up in an efficiency apartment in the rear corner, from which the only opened up facing the alley. The sniper team planned to take up an elevated position on one of the businesses on the opposite side of the alley. They found a flat roof about fifty yards downrange. Rooftops were not among the sniper's favorite places to be, but nothing else was going to work tonight. Considering the layout of the apartment and the limited sight lines afforded them in the alley, it was their only choice. They slipped into position without incident and settled in for the duration.

Radio updates from the negotiators let everyone know there was still no response from the subject. Perimeter officers reported seeing shadows on the shades, hinting he was still inside. The sniper watched the door. The jalousie vents were closed, but light was visible through the frosted glass. Occasionally, a passing silhouette would betray the presence of the subject inside.

Below them, other team members were getting situated. The sniper caught a flash of movement along a hedgerow near the target building. He swung a pair of binoculars in that direction and picked up the figure of Taz. He was doing his scouting pass around the building, making detailed notes to supplement what Patrol had provided. The sniper had seen him do this on previous callouts, but was a little surprised to see Taz working so close this time.

As he watched, the sniper suddenly saw Taz dive for cover behind a telephone pole. Almost simultaneously, Surfer said, "Door's open." The sniper dropped the binos and slid in behind his riflescope. He brought the glass to bear on the building. There, standing silhouetted in the doorway was their subject. The door was completely open, and the subject's hands were hidden beyond the doorframe. Assessing the scene, the sniper also noticed the pole Taz was trying to hide behind was only ten feet or so from the door. He was caught in space with only minimal cover between him and a possibly armed subject.

Surfer was seeing the same thing. "He's trapped. There's nothing close for him to retreat to." Although they couldn't make out the words, the sniper team could hear the subject yelling something at Taz. They could see him pointing at the scout who was trying to disappear behind that pole. "He knows Taz is there." The sniper agreed with Surfer's assessment. Question was, what will he do about it? "I can't see his hands. Watch his hands." The sniper was concerned about the subject and the shotgun he was supposed to have close by. He knew help was on the way, but the sniper had no idea how soon they would arrive. His headset was buzzing with frantic sounding radio traffic as the rest of the team was reacting. He sensed movement next to him as Surfer rolled into position behind his own rifle, and brought it on target.

"I'm on him," was Surfer confirming his status. The sniper backed the power down on his scope to allow him a wider view of the subject standing in the doorway. His hands were still hidden behind the frame, and he was still mouthing something at Taz.

"If he shows me a gun, I'm going to kill him," the sniper hissed as he locked in on the subject. His crosshairs settled on the subject's face, and his finger hovered over his trigger. Thousands of trigger pulls in training told him exactly how much pressure he could safely apply at this point. He was halfway there. Surfer simply answered, "Roger that."

For a long moment, time slowed, as the subject, Taz, and the sniper all seemed to wait for someone else to make the first move. The wrong move would set in motion a rapid exchange of gunfire and sudden death. The sniper felt his pulse pounding in his cheek against the stock of his weapon. The voice in his head was coaching him through his fundamentals.

Rifle firm against the shoulder.

Sight picture, sight alignment.

Breathe. Smooth, steady.

Stare at the crosshairs.

He never saw the arrest team turn the corner of the building and challenge the subject. All he saw in his tight visual circle was the subject look to his right, hesitate for a moment as he contemplated his next move, then throw up empty hands and step out of the apartment. The sniper followed him as the subject went face down on the ground and was quickly swarmed by armed men dressed in black. It was only then that he relaxed and again became aware of the world around him.

On the ground below, the subject had been cuffed and whisked away by part of the team. The remainder lined up and swept into the apartment to clear it. The all clear came from the team leader within minutes. With that, the sniper and his partner set about securing their gear and withdrawing.

Back at the command post, the team gathered around for their ritual debriefing. Each officer was given an opportunity to talk about his involvement and critique his performance. The sniper only half listened to most of the talk until the entry team leader spoke. He said they had recovered the subject's loaded shotgun propped up alongside the doorway. Additional ammunition was in the apartment. The sniper knew this meant, as the subject stood in the doorway, his hand was hovering inches away from his weapon. He had made a choice not to grab it or point it at Taz. His choice had saved his life. The sniper went home, knowing how close he had come to having to take it.

* * * * * * * * * * * *

It was a Sunday morning, about six months later. The sniper was reading the Sunday paper and killing time waiting for the start of the football game. In the local section, a front-page story caught his attention. Apparently, an individual had gotten on a city bus with a large shopping bag. As the bus went along its downtown route, the individual pulled a shotgun out of the bag. According to witnesses, he never said a word as he placed the gun against the back of the head of a passenger seated in front of him. With the squeeze of the trigger, he violently ended the life of a stranger, an innocent man sitting next to his wife. Then, while the rest of the passengers reacted to the thunderous report and the ensuing screams, the individual placed the gun under his chin and blew his own brains out.

The sniper was struck by the senseless nature of the incident. He read the story aloud to his wife, as she stood in the kitchen. When he said the shooter's name, he felt a nagging twinge of recognition. There was something familiar about it. Where did he know him? Nothing in the news story provided additional clues. The sniper was about to miss the feeling when it suddenly clicked. He had seen the name before. He knew the subject.

Six months earlier, his face was framed in the sniper's crosshairs. The sniper held his life and future at the end of a four-pound trigger. Circumstances had spared his life that night. Now, he had murdered a stranger, ruined the lives of untold others, and ended his own pitiful existence with a self-inflicted gunshot.

The sniper's heart sank. In an instant, he felt a hot blend of anger, sorrow, and frustration. He blamed himself, thinking, if only he had shot the individual that night six months ago. He felt responsible for the life of a stranger and accountable to his surviving widow. He felt so many things in that moment, but knew most were wrong. His rational side knew what happened on that bus was beyond his control, and certainly not his fault. As that man stood in his doorway that night, he did nothing to justify being shot by the sniper. As much as his emotional side wished for a chance to turn back the clock, he knew ethically, morally and legally, he had done the right thing. The decision made that night was the correct one, the only one. It was never his choice to make.

Still, to this day, there are those private moments when the sniper allows his mind to wander, and he finds himself back on that rooftop, feeling the pressure on the trigger, staring at the crosshairs, and he wonders about the shot not taken.

ACKNOWLEDGEMENTS

I am what I am because of where I've been. I have been fortunate to spend time in the company of a lot of great men and one great woman. Their influences and friendships have made me the person I am today, and I owe each one of them so very much.

Julie has been my best friend and biggest fan from the beginning. Snipercraft would not have existed without her support and participation. Life wouldn't be nearly as much fun without her around to share it. Here I am showing off for her again.

Mike Preston has been my reliable partner and sidekick. You couldn't ask for a more trust worthy companion, or a better friend.

Richard Morey has committed countless hours of his life to helping me. He is selfless, humble and an honorable man. I value his friendship more than words can convey.

Ed Gross is another great friend, who shares a commitment to the sniper community and to his friends. It has been a pleasure knowing him these past ten years.

There are dozens more, and I don't want to forget any of them. Each, in his way, has enriched me by sharing a part of his life and experiences with me. To Brian Sain, John Simpson, Paul Renkas, Russ Clagett, Jim Main, Johnny Gilmer, Chris Savard, and Dave Grossman, I want to say a heartfelt thank you. You are my heroes, and I consider it an honor to have spent time in your company.

There are dozens more, but I won't bore readers with an interminable list of names. You guys know who you are, and hopefully, you know what you mean to me. Thanks for being there.

FORWARD

The use of police "snipers" is a contemporary one in the history of law enforcement. Depending on your definition, they have been utilized for less than a generation. Only in the last decade have individual officers and agencies really begun in earnest to professionalize this critical aspect of the tactical response. The snipers who are deployed by many agencies in this country are the finest ever fielded. Others, unfortunately, are still struggling to achieve this level of professionalism for a host of reasons.

It can certainly be said that the education and development process is current and ongoing and has not been without significant lessons learned with every success and failure from the law enforcement response. Derrick Bartlett, one of the foremost-recognized sniper instructors, continues to forge down the path toward tactical enlightenment for the specialist called the "Police Sniper."

I met Derrick a decade ago after receiving a reference from a police sniper in Anchorage, Alaska. At the time, I had been instructing police snipers in New England for three years and was actively seeking out information on actual law enforcement incidents for instructional purposes. What I found was that this material was very difficult to obtain and there was no effective network or way to interact with the tactical law enforcement community for this purpose.

The officer, who had seen my national request, referred me to Derrick and told me "with what you're doing, you just have to contact him" and that Snipercraft would be an excellent resource for such professional exchanges. He was right.

My initial phone call to Snipercraft resulted in a very satisfactory exchange of useful information and resources. Here was an organization that had an expressed mission to "enhance the level of proficiency and professionalism of the police sniper through education and information sharing."

I found the Snipercraft organization was very effective at doing this, not the least of which was a regularly-issued, insightful newsletter on police sniper-related topics, events, training and resources.

Ultimately, this led to my attending a Snipercraft training session in Florida with one of my team members. I strongly believe that "a good teacher is a good student," an old Oriental saying. I was to learn that Derrick also had an affinity for the wisdom of the East, and was more "like-minded" than I had anticipated. We had read many of the same books, shared similar experiences, and came to many of the same conclusions, beliefs, and convictions.

What I found in Derrick was a professional, deeply dedicated, and concerned police sniper instructor. I was impressed that when he said something, he did so in an honest, thoughtful and deliberate way. When he had something to say, he said it once and meant it completely and sincerely.

When instructing, he readily shared his personal life experiences and those of many other officers who have shared information with him. His concern was evident for the officers who had been chosen for this difficult and challenging tactical specialty.

It became obvious that he cared deeply about helping other officers who might benefit from the experience of others who had "been there." Through all of this, I found him to be thoughtful, respectful and humble – a consummate professional who taught from the heart. This is sometimes a rare commodity within the vast circle of law enforcement instructors.

My reason for qualifying this particular police sniper and instructor is to accurately reflect the foundation from which he has become an author on the Police Sniper. His first book, *Snipercraft: The Art of the Police Sniper*, has been well received, and now his second effort, *Staring at the Crosshairs*, is much anticipated.

Derrick continues on his intense quest to root out the truth for and about the professional law enforcement sniper. In fact, the contents of his books are an accurate reflection of Derrick Bartlett himself and also his numerous and varied efforts to assist the professional law enforcement specialist. He continues to have his finger on the pulse of the law enforcement sniper community.

Reading *Staring at the Crosshairs*, is likened to spending time at a Snipercraft training session, receiving the quarterly newsletter, *Sniper*, and attending the premier annual police sniper event, SniperWeek, all rolled into one.

Staring at the Crosshairs continues to reveal Derrick's refreshing departure from the technical manuals that abound and many of the other sniper books that have sprung up everywhere in the last decade. His work fills a gap that only experience and lessons learned from actual incidents can fulfill.

What one can find within its pages are a wealth of shared police experiences that can and do affect any police sniper, in any municipality or jurisdiction, and the personal and professional insights into the world of tactical police operations as seen only through "sniper's eyes."

Derrick sometimes presents as an operator, sometimes an instructor, but always as a witness and analyst of the tactical world. His latest offering is a pool of collective information and knowledge of what works and what doesn't work. What police snipers can and can't do, suggestions for their growth, and guidance for professional development.

The new book takes up where the first one left off. There seems to be no end of relevant material pertinent to the police sniper. Personal experiences and actual incidents continually appear, providing rich sources for objective reflection and frank analysis that ultimately influence the police mission and training. As is often said, sometime the truth is stranger than fiction.

Derrick, once again, weaves his personal knowledge and informed opinion throughout the book. He explores each area in a no-nonsense way, using critical thinking and common sense to convey his opinions on each. He doesn't shy away from the tough issues that are part and parcel of the police sniper's world. He offers his experience and candid opinions on a plethora of topics. He does so with conviction and yet with the tempered understanding and the appropriate gravity deserving of the matter.

These issues are the same ones that specialists are dealing in and coming to terms with every day in the field. It is the reality of special operations work in law enforcement and deserving of direct analysis and frank discussion.

Derrick's pragmatic approach clearly and plainly frames each case with logic and insight that comes from years of experience and insight collected through the exchange of shared experiences and collective knowledge from within the law enforcement special operations community.

These are the truths known to police specialists in the field, doing the job of saving and safeguarding life. This information is for every police officer, team leader, tactical commander and police administrator who wants to benefit from the insight gained and "lessons learned" through actual field experiences and from those in the arena. His books are highly recommended and significant resources for agencies charged with a tactical mission.

I'm an active police sniper and team leader. For many years, I've been teaching others in law enforcement the art and military science of precision shooting and police sniping. *Snipercraft: The Art of the Police Sniper* and *Staring at the Crosshairs* are "must reads" for my students.

Derrick continues to be of service to law enforcement and the police sniper community through the creation and sustained efforts of the Snipercraft organization, newsletter, training events, and now with his second effort in print.

As if that is not enough, he also chooses to offer more service through his participation in the American Sniper Association (ASA). He has much to be proud of and the police community much to be grateful for.

The tactical law enforcement community continues to go through this maturation process, sometimes painful, sometimes with unseen, quiet confidence and yet other times in spectacular fashion. Snipercraft and Derrick Bartlett have very much been a part of that process.

As a result, the professional sniper continues to reach higher levels of professionalism, operational readiness and refinement in response to an ever more violent and sophisticated criminal element in our society. No longer an idle and distant threat, global terrorism has struck at the heart of America and is living amongst us. The law enforcement sniper of the future does not have a choice. They will need to be ready to face any new evil that threatens our world.

For those of us dedicated to being professional law enforcement snipers and sniper instructors, the text of this book will ring true. Many of us have dedicated our lives to continually becoming the best that we can be in our field.

Some have taken on the responsibility to teach the police sniper and share the knowledge and experience gleaned through police, military and civilian sources and experiences. Those of us who have been involved in the evolution of this part of police work continue to shape the police sniper community and the free society that it serves.

There is a motto the US Marine Corps uses to express their Honor, Courage, and commitment to duty – Semper Fidelis. It's Latin for "always faithful." If you are on the path and new to this discipline, take heed and learn from those who have gone before you. Your job is to save and safeguard precious human life. Continue to learn, grow, and be ready. Take your job seriously, not yourself. Be always faithful in your commitment, because when SWAT needs help, they "call their snipers."

Should you find yourself reading *Staring at the Crosshairs* and catch yourself acknowledging the contents—good for us. The community has become stronger, better, and as a result, continues to improve. Because you've taken a stand and made a difference with your service, our brother officers, our way of life and our world are a little safer. Semper Fi.

There is an old Oriental expression: *There are many paths up the mountain, but once at the top the view of the moon is the same.* Climb every mountain.

Edward F. Gross
Director - Crosshairs Inc.
VP – American Sniper Association

INTRODUCTION

As I sit down at the keyboard to start this project, it's hard to believe it has been five years since my first book. The time has gone by so fast, and I have grown so much in the interim. That is what motivates me now to start this book. I have seen a lot, done more, and learned many new and important things. This is information I have to share with you.

As with the first book, this will not be a "how-to" manual. There are still plenty of authors out there filling that void. Besides, there is nothing new in the way of ballistic charts, fundamentals, or stalking techniques I can offer to make this book unique in that regard. Let someone else assemble notes they took at sniper school and publish them. This book is different, because it is about what I know, what I believe, and why. It is directed to snipers and to the people given the responsibility of supervising them. I plan to share with you things I think are important for snipers and supervisors to know about themselves and their job. I have included a few rants, but they come with the rationale to support them. You'll find articles, anecdotes, essays and stream of consciousness notations. It is based on what I know, what I have seen, and what I have experienced. Look at this as a verbal scrapbook filled with bits and pieces of information I have accumulated over the years, most professional, some personal.

Hopefully, most of you have read my first book. (For those of you who haven't, shame on you. Rush out and buy a few copies today!) Forgive me if I repeat some things from that book for the benefit of those who didn't. It is important the new reader clearly understands what I believe, and why. However, I will try to keep it to a minimum.

Let me offer a brief recap of my history, for the benefit of any new readers. I became a police officer in Illinois in 1980. I was recruited for the SWAT team two years later. Early on, I gravitated to the sniper rifle and volunteered for the position. I've been married to a long gun ever since. In 1990, I decided I needed a change in scenery and climate. As a result, I joined the Fort Lauderdale Police Department. Less than eighteen months later, I tried out for, and made, the SWAT team again. When the team leaders found out I was formally trained in the fine art of sniping, I was drafted to fill a vacancy. In the years since then, I have had the privilege of training with some of the finest snipers in the special operations world. I have also deployed on a wide variety of real-world missions.

1993 was the official start of Snipercraft. Initially, it was a vehicle to facilitate hosting a sniper competition. It quickly grew from a one shot affair to an international training event and tournament. We are now in our second decade of operation with no end in sight. Sniper-Week is recognized throughout the community as the "Olympics of Sniping."

We have also established a diversified training program, which has given me the opportunity to travel the country, instructing thousands of snipers and supervisors in classes, seminars and lectures. It has also given me the chance to spend time in the company of instructors and snipers, picking their brains and learning from their experiences.

My training and experience don't qualify me as a Grand Master Sniper. I will not insult anyone by claiming to know the best way, right way, or only way to do this job. I don't claim to have all the answers. I only claim a unique set of life experiences, which may hold information you will find enlightening. All I ask from you is to approach this book with an open mind and a willingness to listen to another sniper's opinion.

I am not one to mince words. I have little tolerance for political correctness when it comes to this trade. I am known as a person who says what he believes, and believes in what he says.

I believe sniping is an art, not a science. There is no perfect combination of rifle, ammunition, optics, uniform, and tactics that will work for every sniper in the field. Each one of you has to spend time personalizing your "sniper package." Little by little, you have to accumulate the customized elements which fit you best and make you the most efficient sniper you can be.

To me, sniping is a martial art, not unlike karate or kung fu. It is a discipline requiring an equal amount of dedication, study, and constant practice to master. With mastery, comes great expectation and great responsibility.

I believe many snipers are badly trained, poorly equipped, improperly used, and under appreciated. Far too many supervisors and administrators seem to learn what they know about snipers from the movies. A few snipers fall into that trap as well. Education is needed by all parties to correct this. If you are willing to learn, there are plenty of reputable resources and training venues available to you.

I believe some snipers join our ranks because they like the toys and think the title is cool, but don't really want to do the work. Being a sniper is a special calling, requiring an individual who understands what is at stake and accepts the responsibility. If you don't share our dedication and passion, you don't deserve to be among us. This is not a game.

I believe the career of a sniper is a journey of experience and enlightenment. Every day should teach you something new. Every callout, every training day, every book, video, school, should all reveal another step in your development. This growth should continue as long as you are carrying the rifle and bearing the title. Consider this book a step on your journey.

This book does not represent the best, only or right way to be a sniper. It is simply one sniper's humble opinion.

> "To be a Master is to be in a constant state of becoming. For that which is not moving toward something is moving away from it." —Chiun, Master of Sinanju

THE DIRTY LITTLE SECRET

Everybody has one—that skeleton in the closet, that dark secret you wish wasn't there. Law enforcement agencies have one, as well.

The saying goes, "When people need help, they call the police. When the police need help, they call SWAT." For the most part, the police never want to admit they need help. SWAT is a tool of last resort, an admission of failure. The "real cops" couldn't get it done, so they have to call in the prima donnas. Maybe it isn't that way everywhere, but it happens more than it should.

As if that wasn't bad enough, inside the SWAT community there resides another dirty little secret. They work in the shadows, waiting for a chance to ambush an unsuspecting target. By their very nature, they are deceptive, devious, sneaky, hard to trust. Worse, it's hard to admit they are working for us.

We try to conceal their existence. We call them marksmen or sharpshooters, if we refer to them at all. Sometimes, we try to be obscure by calling them Sierra teams, or we get creative with laughable euphemisms like Long Range Tactical Interventionist.

We don't train them or support them, for that is an admission we may someday need them. Our hope is, there will always be another way. Anything is better than turning them loose on our citizens. On operations, we keep them in check, limiting their discretion. Granting them authority to engage could be viewed as a license to kill. Decisions to use force should be left to levelheaded administrators who can see the big picture and appreciate the ramifications of their actions.

Still, when the time comes, they answer the call to duty and carry out their assignment. They succeed in the face of overwhelming obstacles. Unwanted and unappreciated—until that crucial moment when they are the only option, the last resort. Suddenly, everyone is aware of their presence and all eyes are on them. They do their job, and then return to obscurity, while others take the credit.

They are a necessary evil to some. To others, they resemble that fire extinguisher, stored in a sealed cubicle with "In case of emergency, break glass." They are the tactical black sheep. They are the relatives no one wants to talk about. They are snipers, law enforcement's dirty little secret.

A CHAPTER FOR SUPERVISORS

Even if you have no real desire to read the rest of this book, I hope I can have your attention for a few pages to pass on some information specifically for you.

I am not a supervisor, and I don't pretend to be able to tell you how to supervise your sniper team. However, I have the advantage of having seen sniper teams all over the country. I have had a close look at good programs and bad programs. As a result, I can tell you, with confidence, how a successful sniper team should be supervised and why. The choice to follow my advice is yours.

I believe no one is born knowing how to supervise a sniper team. Earning stripes, bars or becoming a team leader doesn't automatically equip you with the skills and knowledge necessary to be an effective sniper supervisor. A smart supervisor realizes this and takes steps to correct it. Therefore, my first recommendation would be, every person who is tasked with the responsibility of supervising a sniper team should attend a sniper school. The intent is not to make you into a sniper. Learning to see the world with "sniper's eyes" will give you a unique perspective. It will help you understand how snipers are trained to think, move and act. It will give you an appreciation for their capabilities and limitations. It will also give you invaluable, hands-on experience with the tools of the trade. Nothing will give you the same respect for snipers as eating dirt with them.

There are also classes being offered in different places geared specifically for sniper team leaders. Attend them. These classes will help you in areas like designing training programs, training documentation, purchasing, and operational command issues. More specialized information from additional sources will only help you be a better supervisor.

If your team doesn't already have them, write up a complete SOP for the sniper team. The policy should cover aspects like the team's mission, selection of personnel, command structure, training and qualifications, operational directives, and deadly force policy. Care must be taken to avoid making the policy too detailed or restrictive. It should act as a framework for the program, without being too rigid. If you are unsure how to accomplish this, don't be afraid to consult agencies that have already written policies, or contact the American Sniper Association. A sample guideline is also included in the Appendix.

Take the time to select good personnel. Not every SWAT officer is cut out for the job of a sniper, so don't settle for putting just anyone in the position. Look at the desirable criteria and use a uniform selection process to choose the best candidates.

Buy the team good equipment. (This will be a recurring theme, so get used to hearing it.) As the supervisor, you represent the liaison between your snipers and the upper administration. When they come to you asking for equipment, you have to be the salesman who pitches their requests to the bean counters. You will have to be able to justify purchases that run counter to the lowest bidder practices agencies usually follow. It will fall on your shoulders to make them understand the differences between match grade ammunition and regular hunting ammo, and why the agency has to spend more money to buy the right stuff. Of course, you will be hard-pressed to make the necessary sales pitch if you don't have the facts. So, your responsibility includes doing homework and research. You have to learn what equipment is available, what it costs, and where it can be purchased.

Send your personnel to school and insist they maintain a high level of ongoing training. Certified training is a necessity for snipers. It is a good foundation for their job skills. It builds confidence in their abilities. It provides protection against possible litigation as a result of any actions your snipers may take in the future. Sending them into the operational arena without documented, certified training from a reputable training provider is inexcusable and negligent on your part.

Ongoing, in-service training is equally important, for all of the same reasons. Because you are the supervisor, it will be your responsibility to design a structured training program, make sure it is conducted, and maintain all of the proper documentation. There are standards for training, addressing content and hours, available from ASA, which you can use as the guidelines for setting up your program. It will be up to you to establish the program and fight against the inevitable cutbacks and budget constraints to maintain the level of training in the future.

It is advisable you take an active role in their training. Go out with them to the range and shoot. Spend time working with them as they practice fieldcraft and tactics, as well. Learn how to interact with them on callouts.

The most visible gauge of your effectiveness as the sniper team leader will be your management of sniper deployments. In an operational environment, your snipers will be called upon to act as a component in a tactical, problem-solving matrix. You will act as the liaison, coordinating their efforts with the negotiators, entry teams and administrators to best effect. A close working relationship with your sniper team, and a clear understanding of their mission capabilities will be very important at this stage. If you have done a good job as team leader, your team will do a good job. If your leadership has been lacking, your failings will be reflected in their performance.

The impact of poor supervision in a tactical operation is illustrated in an incident from the Midwest a few years ago. The team in question responded to a barricaded subject who had fired shots at officers. The Chief of Police and Special Operations Bureau Commander showed up and took command of the scene. After a couple of hours on scene, the Chief told his team leaders they were going home for some sleep, and ordered them to do nothing until he returned. His incredulous team could only take cover and settle in for the night. He returned later, checked out the situation, and was advised the team was preparing to breach the door and make an entry. The Chief told them to stand down, and then told the team leaders he was leaving again to attend a promotional ceremony. By this time, the team had been on call for over 12 hours. Once again, he told them to take no action until he returned. They returned about three hours later. Action was delayed while negotiators appeared to make headway with the subject. The Chief and commander told the team they were leaving for lunch, and once again told the team leaders to take no action on their own until they returned. By the time they did return, the subject inside had committed suicide. The cumulative effect on the team was demoralizing, to say the least.

The success or failure of your sniper program will fall directly on you. After all, you are responsible for the team's structure, selection, training, equipment, and utilization. Your influence on the program is undeniable. Be a positive influence. Understand your role and endeavor to be the best sniper team leader you can be. Don't be satisfied, as so many team leaders are, to simply "be in charge" of the sniper element. I have seen that approach up close, and I know how demoralizing that can be for the people under your command. There is more to being an effective supervisor than management. Lead wisely. Know when to command, when to delegate, and when to ask for help.

NOT YOUR USUAL SWAT CALL

On the morning of August 1, 1966, Charles Whitman walked out onto the clock tower observation deck at the University of Texas. From his barricaded vantage point, he proceeded to shoot at targets of opportunity on the campus below. In less than ninety minutes, he would kill 12 people, and wound another 30.

As police resources responded, they immediately found themselves at a disadvantage. Not only did Whitman's position provide him a wide kill zone, and ample ballistic protection, he also possessed weapons superior to the handguns and shotguns available to the police. Whitman's rampage wasn't ended until two Austin city police officers were able to get up on the observation deck and confront him face to face.

What happened that day in Texas should have served as a wake up call to law enforcement agencies worldwide. This incident, however, was treated as an anomaly, a once in a lifetime event which couldn't possibly happen again. Whitman's use of strategy, superior firepower and positioning stymied police resources. Still, the law enforcement community has chosen to ignore the lessons of the past, rather than learn from them.

More than thirty years later, agencies everywhere are still reassuring themselves by saying, "It was an isolated incident. It can't happen here." A philosopher once told us, "Those who refuse to learn from the past are doomed to repeated it." Ever since that August afternoon in Austin, criminal snipers have been carrying out similar attacks, and in most cases, police response has not changed. The result has been casualties, both civilian and police personnel.

Louisiana — A criminal sniper attacks police headquarters, and a downtown hotel, eventually killing nine, including five police officers, and wounding over a dozen more.

Indiana — A sniper shoots and kills a police officer responding to a shots fired complaint in a trailer park.

Mississippi — From a sniper hide in a shopping center, a concealed shooter killed one, and wounded ten before killing himself.

Australia — Seven die and nineteen are wounded by a sniper hiding in a landscaped median.

England — Part sniper, part active shooter, this individual terrorized a neighborhood for nearly six hours, while killing 15.

Arkansas — A pair of snipers attacks their school, orchestrating an ambush to kill five, including a teacher, and wound twelve more.

Washington, DC — A pair of snipers paralyze a portion of the country during their three-week campaign of calculated death and terror. This unprecedented pair of hit and run snipers kills 10 people before they are finally arrested.

Make no mistake about it. A sniper incident is not your usual call for service. If you and your agency approach it as such, the consequences will be tragic. Nor is it the rare, isolated event you may think it is.

Administrators, tactical team leaders and supervisors should be aware of the following points regarding criminal sniper incidents:

• A criminal sniper incident can happen anywhere, anytime. History offers no statistical protection to any certain type of jurisdiction. Sniper incidents are not limited by country, state or city limits. This type of incident has victimized everything from huge metropolitan areas to rural stretches of highway. This means your town is a potential target for the sniper incident that will take place somewhere tomorrow. Thousands of sniping incidents have taken place since Whitman. Only those resulting in body counts make the news. In this age of jaded media and viewers, only large body counts make the national news programs. As a result, the majority of these incidents go under-reported and unknown. Many seemingly-random homicides may actually be sniper victims.

• Criminal snipers fall into one of two broad categories. The Hit & Run Sniper is the more prevalent. Every call of random shots fired is a possible Hit & Run Sniper. These individuals take up a position of concealment, fire a few shots, and then withdraw, or move to another hide. Their targets may be buildings, streetlights, or passing cars. In some cases, they will attack people. As people or police begin to recognize his presence and respond to it, the Hit & Run Sniper will retreat. His escape will allow him to attack again, at a time and place of his choosing. Mark Essex is a prime example of the Hit & Run Sniper. The Beltway shooters elevated this tactic to a new and frightening level.

The other category is the Barricaded Sniper. This is the one who makes the Six O'clock News. This sniper sets up his firing position, attacks his targets, and is still there when the police arrive. He has made a decision to continue his killing spree until you find a way to stop him. He represents the most dangerous threat police officers will ever face.

• Preparation is the essential element necessary for a safe and effective response. This means developing plans ahead of time for the probability of having to deal with a sniper call, and taking the time to practice them. While the bullets are flying and the bodies are falling is the wrong time to be making up a strategy. Recognize the probability. A sniper incident is going to happen. You have no control over when or where. However, it is going to happen. It is your responsibility to be ready and equipped to handle it quickly, safely and effectively.

• Potential sniper encounters should be anticipated in any of the following scenarios:

1. Riot situations and events of civil unrest. Some individuals take advantage of the chaotic circumstances surrounding riots to take pot shots at the crowds or emergency personnel on the scene. Review the after action reports of any large civil disturbance, and you will find stories of firefighters and police officers who have come under fire from undetected snipers.

2. Dignitary and protection details. Every time your agency is tasked with providing security for a visiting dignitary, politician, celebrity, or other high-profile individual, you run the risk of someone trying to kill your protectee. Remember, two of the most famous assassinations in recent American history, were perpetrated in this fashion. Both Martin Luther King and John F. Kennedy were killed by snipers. Abortion clinic doctors have recently been the

targets for this type of sniper as well.

3. Ambushes. Planned attacks on police officers have become an alarming trend. Many of the most recent sniper incidents have been carefully executed ambushes of police personnel. The standard tactic is to make a bogus call to make police respond to a specific location. As the unsuspecting officers arrive on scene, they are systematically attacked. A graphic demonstration of this tactic was employed a couple of years ago in Texas, where three officers were killed, one by one, as they arrived to handle a phony domestic dispute call.

4. SWAT Calls. Special Operations teams are accustomed to responding to a hostage situation, or a barricaded subject. The standard response in those circumstances is to contain and contact. The culprit is usually passive and defensive, and content to negotiate. On rare occasions, the culprits have turned offensive, actively attacking responders in their containment positions. At that point, standard SWAT logic goes out the window, and a different approach needs to be adopted.

5. Random acts of terror. One of the major lessons learned from the Beltway incident was the impact an extended hit and run sniper campaign could have on an area. The presence of a mystery shooter on the loose basically shut down several states, tying up resources and altering the way people lived their daily lives. As a result, the paralyzing effect of a sniper campaign as a terror tool certainly was not lost on those predisposed to attacks on civilians. This may be the terror tool of choice in the near future.

These are not the only situations that may lead to a sniper incident. Crime is limited only by the imaginations of the people perpetrating it. Tomorrow, a new sniper may create his own initiating event.

• There is a distinctive attack profile associated with the criminal sniper. First, a sniper attack is rarely a spontaneous event. The perpetrators do not simply wake up one morning, grab a rifle, and go on a shooting rampage. On the contrary, the majority of sniper incidents are the final product of extensive planning and practice. The culprits have been known to do site visits to choose their kill zone. They have purchased weapons and ammunition in advance. Many have done extra training, specifically for their "mission." A number of them have written about their intentions in journals and letters, well in advance of the actual event.

With the possible exception of a SWAT incident that evolves from a domestic call, there are usually no hostages involved. As a result, there are no demands from the shooter, and negotiations are pointless. His agenda is strictly offensive. Stopping to talk takes away from shooting time.

Usually, the shooter does not personally know his targets. They are faceless strangers chosen at random by where they are, or with whom they associate on the day he initiates his attack. The exception to this is the deliberately chosen assassination target.

• Criminal snipers attack with a plan. In looking over the hundreds of documented sniper incidents from the last decade, a method to their madness appears.

The sniper will choose a kill zone. As pointed out earlier, many snipers pick out locations familiar to them, or they have taken the time to actually scout out a perspective kill zone. Charles Whitman was familiar with the campus of his university. He knew where to position himself to best take advantage of his target-rich environment. Others since have followed suit.

The sniper will use some method to draw targets into his kill zone. In Jonesboro, AR, the snipers pulled a fire alarm to bring their targets out to the playground. Others have set fires or made false 911 calls. One favored tactic has been around for a hundred years. Snipers have been known to wound one person, and then lay in wait to attack anyone attempting to rescue or render aid to them.

At some point in time, the sniper makes a determination to stay and continue to kill, or withdraw undetected. Sometimes, this decision is made on the spot. Usually, though, the sniper knew when he left home whether he was planning to come back.

• At the beginning, the sniper has the upper hand. He is initiating the attack at a time and place of his choosing. He has scouted the area and knows the approaches and escape routes. He is familiar with your expected response practices and is anticipating your every move. (Anyone doubting this has only to read some of the interviews granted by surviving snipers after their surrender. They knew what they were doing, and what they expected the police to do. They were able to predict and counter most police tactics as they were employed.) He is operating from a position of concealment and cover. He sees responding police units long before they can see him. He is often equipped with weapons that give him ballistic superiority to anything the police may have in their holsters. The police will just be more targets of opportunity.

• There is a tendency to underestimate the sniper. Admittedly, barricading oneself in a building and shooting at everything that moves is an act of complete madness. It is not something a rational human being is noted for doing. But don't make the strategic gaffe of thinking this person can be dealt with like your average nut case. Crazy does not equal stupid. That person may well be better trained, better equipped, and better prepared for this encounter than any of your responding personnel. To treat him as anything less, because you doubt his mental capabilities, invites disaster, because it gives him yet another tactical advantage.

So, with these facts in mind, what should law enforcement do to handle the next major sniper incident? They should begin with a pro-active approach to the potential problem. Take the time to learn from the snipers of the past. Books and articles written about the Who's Who of sniping will reveal a wealth of valuable lessons. Today, we have the advantage of studying the cases of Charles Whitman, Jimmy Essex, James Kristian, Julian Knight, Brenda Spencer, and others like them, from the last 30 years. The attack profiles and tactics of the shooters continue to be repeated; likewise, the responses and mistakes made by law enforcement. These case studies provide a textbook for all of law enforcement to study in preparation for their confrontation. Become a student of history.

Agencies must establish policies dictating responses of all involved resources. Such policies are already in place for major accidents, natural disasters, and large events. A sniper incident, especially a barricade, requires the same level of involvement and coordination of responding resources. Police, fire, EMS and others may all be called in during a major sniper call. If no policy is in place today, then you will be making it up on the fly tomorrow.

Plan for the worst-case scenarios, and train for them on a departmental level. It may be a major task to coordinate, and it will be costly and time-consuming. However, training is the only safe place to try out the elements of your proposed plan and make corrections. Training is the time when mistakes can be made without sacrificing lives. Without a planned, coordinated response, which has been practiced and perfected, the lives of everyone on scene will be at unnecessary risk. Approaching an active criminal sniper cold is inviting catastrophe.

Take special care to properly prepare your patrol personnel. In all sniper incidents, they will be among the first to make contact with the shooter. They will often be counted among the first casualties. They need to know the potential threat they will be facing, and how to respond to safely contain the shooter. They also need to be equipped with weaponry that will give them an equal chance in fighting the sniper. Handguns and shotguns are no match for a barricaded sniper with a scoped rifle.

Develop a structured operational sequence for locating, isolating, and neutralizing the sniper as quickly as possible. This plan will be put into motion by the first responders, but as the incident goes on, it will have to be continued by SWAT personnel. Classroom instruction, provided by qualified and knowledgeable personnel, is the best starting point for this process. Practical exercises help to fine-tune the plan and reinforce the details.

Stop relying on luck. The success of a tactical operation should not hinge on the distribution of good fortune. Your team should win, because it comes to the scene with a superior attitude and a superior state of mind. You prevail, because of superior training, equipment, deployment, tactics and execution. A criminal sniper incident is like nothing else in police work. Safely resolving it requires planning and training. Realizing the probability of such an incident taking place in your jurisdiction, and not taking immediate action to prepare your personnel to handle it, borders on deliberate indifference. The Chief of Police for Austin, Texas, Robert Miles, gave a news conference shortly after the Texas Tower shootings. He sounded almost prophetic when he said, "This could have happened in any city in America, or in the world for that matter."

For the last thirty-plus years, he has been right. The question you have to ask yourself and your agency is, "Are you ready for the next Charles Whitman?"

STILL THE MOST DANGEROUS OPTION

Several years ago, a sharpshooter in the Midwest "saved" an individual from killing himself by shooting the revolver from his hand with a .308 sniper rifle. This was a shot heard throughout the sniper community. Everywhere, snipers, tactical commanders, and departmental administrators debated and discussed the pros and cons of this controversial tactic. Some were impressed with the success in this instance, and felt it was a tactic that merited practice and consideration. Others took a more skeptical stand, realizing the dangers inherent in this course of tactical action.

That shot, that day, was absolutely perfect. Everything went as well as anyone could have hoped. The shot struck the weapon at precisely the right point; the weapon broke apart and was rendered inoperable. The subject holding the gun was unharmed. No bystanders were hurt by flying debris or bullet fragments. And the subject was not carrying a second weapon. He sat quietly and waited until assault team members took him to the ground and into custody.

Of course, the team responsible took full credit for the success of their operation. The sniper claimed to be able to place his shots "within a thirty-secondth of an inch." Pretty amazing when one considers all of the uncontrollable factors that influence a shot. (Strangely, even manufacturers of the finest sniper rifles guarantee no greater than a quarter minute of angle accuracy from their weapons. A minor detail.) He knew exactly where to strike the weapon to make it inoperable, send the parts in a safe direction and did it from 65 yards away. Quite the accomplishment. Do we attribute this to skill, luck, or a fortuitous blend of both?

What else could have happened? On another day, with another sniper shooting at another weapon, how might the story have ended? This particular incident was highly publicized, appearing in local and national news reports. However, other less publicized incidents have met with less perfect results. More on that later.

The idea of keeping an individual from killing himself by shooting at him is frightening, dangerous, and in most states, illegal. Although I have always been very vocal in my opposition to the use of this tactic from the beginning, I felt it was important to conduct an objective study to document the facts, which support our belief. (As good friend, John Simpson, likes to say, "If I can't show you the math, then it is just my opinion.") To accomplish this, members of the American Sniper Association set up a controlled series of tests and recorded our results for analysis. Armed with these facts, plus anecdotal information, decisions regarding the employment of this tactic can be made from a position of knowledge. Our decision to mount this project took on an additional level of urgency after another Midwest agency sniper shot a gun from the hand of a suicidal individual a few months ago.

Ours is not the first test of this type; nor is it the definitive, comprehensive study on the topic. It was not our intention to develop a chart of statistical probabilities for various outcomes. We shot at 20 different weapons. Percentages generated from this sampling would be irrelevant. Instead, the strength of this study comes from a review of the highlights among our test shots. Our tests were intended to collect empirical data, and demonstrate the full spectrum of possible outcomes.

To conduct our tests, we constructed a clamping device. This was a platform made of $5/8$-inch plywood, to which two steel vises were bolted. These would be used to hold the test weapons in place. Certainly, the vise would hold the weapon a lot firmer than any person would grip it, however, for safety purposes, we wanted to control the movement of the weapons after they were impacted by our shots. This control was appreciated after the first firearm discharged on impact.

Foamcore backers were set up on three sides of the clamping device. White butcher paper was suspended between the cardboard panels. These "witness panels" would help us document the flight of any fragments, debris, and bullets.

We fired shots at a variety of weapons, including revolvers, semi-automatic handguns, rifles, and shotguns.

Members of the American Sniper Association and the South Florida Community College Video Productions staff documented the entire test. High-speed videotapes and digital still photographs were taken of each shot and its aftermath.

The shots were taken by snipers from Ft. Lauderdale PD and the Collier County Sheriff's Office. The snipers used bolt-action .308 rifles. The distance was 40 yards. This was done, in part, to help insure accurate shot placement at precise aim points on the targeted weapons. It was also a concession to the safety of the personnel involved in the testing. Anticipating the possibility of flying debris, we didn't want to place the video camera (and the operator), or our shooters, too close.

With everything in place, we began our testing. We started learning lessons of great value from the very outset.

First, we were made aware of the difficulty of placing the perfect shot. Each weapon was held stationary in a clamping device. The shooters fired from supported positions 40 yards away from the weapons. Even under these controlled circumstances, some of the shooters failed to place their first shots exactly on designated aim points. This proved to us that shooting a weapon from a hand, which could be moving in a random fashion, at any practical distance, is as much luck as it is skill. Don't kid yourselves. Such a shot in real life leaves no margin for error.

What follows is a recap of significant findings from our tests:

- Shooting a loaded Interarms .38 revolver in the cylinder, resulted in the cylinder exploding in a shower of metal and lead shrapnel as four rounds detonated. Metal fragments penetrated several witness panels.
- The same results happened when a Colt .38 revolver was shot.
- A loaded and cocked S&W revolver was shot with a frangible round, again targeting the cylinder. The hammer dropped on impact, firing one round while another in the cylinder detonated. The frangible round was used because one manufacturer had insinuated it would work better in this application than a normal jacketed round.
- A .22 Luger was shot in the magazine well. Not surprisingly, the top four rounds in the magazine exploded.
- Firing a single shot that struck just behind the cylinder area of a .22 revolver resulted in two rounds detonating, and the gun ex-

ploding in spectacular fashion. Some of the recovered parts landed as far as 20 yards away.

- Shots fired at a pair of long guns yielded notable results. A Sako 30.06 rifle was shot in the bolt area. The chambered round detonated, blowing a large hole in a witness panel. Examining the weapon, we found that the single round in the magazine had also detonated. A .308 was fired at the chamber area of a full stock, over/under Mossberg shotgun. The gun discharged, and the resulting recoil flung the gun over the witness panels.

- A second shotgun was broken in half by a single round striking it in the chamber.

- A constant in all of the weapons shot was the significant amount of metal spalling and fragmentation. The witness panels clearly captured this consequence of tactical disarmament.

- More than half of the loaded weapons we shot at detonated as a result of being struck.

In a perfect world, on a perfect day, a single shot from a high-powered rifle can surgically remove and neutralize a weapon held in the hand of a suicidal subject. There will be no injuries caused by the bullet fired or secondary missiles. Errant rounds and sympathetic discharges will endanger no bystanders. However, we don't work in a perfect world.

If you or your agency is giving any thought to using tactical disarmament as a tactical option, be aware of the possible consequences and outcomes.

The targeted weapon is probably going to be in motion, and partially obscured by the hand of the person wielding it. The weapon is already a small target. In the case of firearms, the point that needs to be struck in order to completely disable it is even smaller. Failure to disable the weapon with one shot can, and has, caused tragic outcomes.

The sniper will be shooting a frangible, high-speed, lead projectile at a steel object, possibly containing a number of explosive cartridges. When the weapon is struck, there is going to be substantial fragmentation, a mixture of metal and lead. Displaced metal will fly away from the point of impact at all angles, and at speeds in excess of 1000 feet per second. Those fragments will vary in size, but many will be large enough, and traveling fast enough, to lacerate, maim, blind or kill. There will be no way of predicting or controlling the extent, speed or direction of the fragmentation.

In the case of loaded firearms, there is a strong possibility it will discharge after being impacted by a rifle shot. The rounds discharged by the weapon will also depart in unpredictable directions. By firing the shot, the sniper possibly will place everyone in the vicinity at risk of injury or worse, including the person he is trying to "save."

This is not meant to imply something bad will happen when attempting to shoot a weapon from someone's hand. It simply means something bad can happen.

In Oregon, a weapon was shot from the hand of an individual threatening himself and others. The round wounded him and knocked the gun from his right hand. However, as police rushed in, he picked up the still functional gun with his uninjured hand and used it to kill himself.

A robber is Montreal held police at bay by pointing a loaded semi-automatic pistol at his head. The on-scene commander decided to use his snipers to disarm the individual at first opportunity. The round fired, from a distance of 22 meters, went through the magazine well of the weapon. At least one of the rounds in the magazine detonated. The impact, bullet strike and sympathetic detonation resulted in a broken arm, as well as the suicidal robber losing two fingers.

Not learning their lesson the first time, the same team was faced with a suicidal subject a few weeks later. The subject had been firing a rifle randomly in the neighborhood, and trying to entice the police to kill him. A sniper was again ordered to disarm the subject. The sniper waited for an opening and shot the rifle away from the subject when it was pointed at the ground. As the arrest team rushed the subject to take him into custody, he picked the gun up and pointed it at the team. Not sure if the gun was still functional, the sniper felt it necessary to shoot and kill the subject to protect his team.

To this day, that agency in the Midwest still believes their actions were heroic. Even though the commander on scene was recorded saying, "If the sniper screwed up, his career and mine would be over." Not exactly a resounding endorsement for a tactic.

Knowing beforehand the high level of risk involved in employing tactical disarmament, any agency choosing to use this tactic should have an unlimited supply of money on hand. There is no way to guarantee the safety of anyone at the scene of such a shooting. The final outcome of this type of use of force is almost completely random. Avoiding injury or death is simply beyond the control of the shooter. Consider carefully whether or not this is still a viable tactical option. Careers, reputations and lives may be riding on your final decision.

YOU ARE NOT IN CONTROL

At the conclusion of each training event, class and competition, we take time to carefully read the evaluations submitted by students. The feedback we receive is invaluable in helping us fine-tune our program to address the needs of our audience.

After a recent competition, one such evaluation caught our attention. The competitor commented, "The majority of the course was speed-oriented, and precision shooting needs to be added." Apparently, someone missed the point. Every course, in every class, and every competition, is all about precision shooting. It's just not on your terms.

When the pager goes off, the police on scene have determined the situation they are facing is beyond their capabilities. Someone is engaged in actions which conventional police approaches have failed to end. They have called for SWAT. On your arrival, the bad guy is contained, and his access to certain things may be restricted. However, he is in control of most other factors.

He will decide how the situation will end. He will decide whether or not you, your teammates, or any hostages will be placed in imminent danger. He will ultimately decide if he wants to surrender, or force a lethal confrontation.

Which brings us to my point. If and when he decides to initiate a lethal confrontation, it will be at his discretion, not yours. What will then be tested is your ability to fire an accurate shot, quickly and on demand. Is there speed involved? Yes, but it is not separated from the need to be accurate.

The question I have for you is have you prepared for this shot? Taking up a comfortable, prone, bipod position, firing a slow-fire string of shots at a bullseye target, at a known distance, may do wonders for your ego. It may impress your teammates and your boss. However, when the pager goes off, no one at the scene will be the least bit interested in how tight a three round group you can shoot in practice. They won't care about your highest bullseye score last training day. The only thing that will matter at that moment is your ability to deliver one accurate shot, on demand, under pressure, under any circumstances. Can you make that shot? Do you have the confidence that comes from having done it over and over in practice? Can you look through your scope, quartering a partially exposed target that must be shot now, and calm yourself by saying, "I've done this in training. It's no big deal."

Do not delude yourself into believing you will never be faced with a hurried decision and a pressured shot. In recent years, I have been made aware of several incidents, which lead to deadly force confrontations within minutes of the arrival of SWAT elements. There was no time to settle in, get comfortable, and wait for the right time. The bad guy dictated the timing. He made the final decision. And I am sure, he reminded everyone there, they were not in control.

Accept the reality and prepare.

YOU ARE THE ENEMY

Know your enemy—sound advice that has been passed on to warriors for generations. This piece of advice is no less relevant today.

As police officers and SWAT team members, we sometimes underestimate the people we encounter in our daily activities as well as during callouts. We believe everyone to be "just some drunk," or "an irate ex-employee," or some other limiting classification. The danger inherent in doing this is we approach these individuals feeling a bit superior. After all, he can't be as well-trained or equipped as we are; therefore, he can't be much of a threat. Wrong! And that way of thinking will get you or your teammates killed.

Each year, the military of this and other countries releases hundreds of highly-trained and specially-qualified individuals back into civilian life. Around the world, special interest groups, militias, terrorist organizations and others spend time and money training and equipping themselves for confrontations with their perceived enemies. Publications from companies like Paladin Press, Delta Press and others teach anyone, with the money to buy the books, how to build bombs, execute ambushes, conduct surveillances and counter your tactics. Books, videos and websites provide additional training for interested students. Of particular concern to you should be the amount of sniper training that is available to the general public. A visit to any local gun show will give you an idea what kinds of weapons are in the hands of the average citizen, that guy you might later categorize as "just some nut case." Gas masks, body armor, explosives, and night vision are also available to civilians—both good and bad—through any number of avenues.

Recently, an anonymous individual posted a website on the Internet, which dealt with tactics designed to defeat SWAT teams. He systematically listed the SWAT tactic and his ideas for counters. Some of his ideas were completely off base, but others hit too close to home to be ignored. What should be frightening is knowing he is not the only one out there thinking this way.

Your enemy is studying you. He is preparing for confrontations with police and special units. He has learned your tactics. He has emulated your equipment and weaponry. He is motivated by fear and paranoia. He sees you as his enemy. He may be a terrorist from some distant land, or he may be of the homegrown variety. He may be just a guy who knows a few things. Whatever his pedigree, you stand between him and whatever goal he is seeking to accomplish, whether it is robbing a bank, killing a group of strangers, or simply not going back to jail. You are his enemy, he knows you, and he hides among the people you deal with every day.

Know your enemy. Read what he reads. See how he thinks. Learn what he knows. Be prepared to meet him, because he is prepared for you.

> How can any man say what he should do himself,
> if he is ignorant of what his enemy is about?
> —Baron D. M. Shoup

LAW ENFORCEMENT ONLY

This seems like an appropriate point to address this area of contention. Although it is a touchy subject with me, I won't beat it to death here.

Reading postings on websites, emails and other correspondence that comes to my office, there are those persons who take issue with our policy of limiting our services to law enforcement and military personnel only. We have been called elitists, and told how much we are missing out on by not including civilians. Others have berated us, accusing us of conspiring to violate the rights of private citizens while practicing our secret handshakes. They have offered all sorts of rationales for being included in police training events and associations. Some are downright amusing. My favorite was the gentleman who described himself as "a qualified civilian sniper." I wrote back and asked him for a job description. I never got one.

It is true; there are people who are knowledgeable and skilled shooters. In their competitive world, they excel at their sport. Tactical snipers can learn a lot from them. After all, they get a lot more practice working on some of the mechanical skills like reading the wind, or shooting long distances. I encourage snipers to attend competitions and exchange information with the people there. However, there are differences between them and us they have to accept. While there are places and occasions when law enforcement personnel and civilians can mix, there are others where civilians are neither appropriate nor welcome. Police training is for police officers, period. It is not open for debate. Just because someone has an interest is what we are doing, doesn't qualify him to attend. The most hardcore Harley rider in the world is not going to be allowed to attend motor school. Being an avid dog lover is not enough to qualify someone for K-9 training. Sniper schools are no different.

To them, shooting is a sport or a hobby. Their interest in sniping is a curiosity, a Walter Mitty obsession. To us, it is our job. They want to rub shoulders with the pros and convince themselves we have something in common. We are not training to punch holes in paper to score points and win trophies. We are training to win a confrontation involving real life and sudden death. We are training to kill human beings in order to save others. Ours is an arena where the targets sometimes shoot back. It is not the fantasy world of weekend warriors. For us, it is about real bullets, real bad guys, and real blood.

Having talked with these people on many occasions, I know there is little I can say to make them understand why they can't come over to play. But I am comfortable with my decision to exclude them.

Again referring to the DC sniper incident, during that time period, interest in the so-called "sniper subculture" reached an all time high. Reporters and talk show hosts contacted me easily 20 times a day over that three-week stretch. Some were sincerely interested in finding out factual information about professional snipers and our reaction to the event. Others were calling to express their righteous indignation that organizations like ours existed. They honestly felt we were somehow responsible for the actions of people like those then unknown shooters. How dare we promulgate such activity! However, when I was able respond by telling them we were a professional organization, which provides training and support for police and military personnel only, it instantly took the wind out of their sails. You couldn't argue with preparing the men and women who do this for a living.

I have always joked with friends and students about my "60 Minutes" nightmare. In it, I am running for my car, with Mike Wallace and a camera crew chasing me. I have a newspaper hiding my face, muttering "No comment," as Wallace is asking me, "Isn't it true you provided training for the man who used a rifle to kill a dozen children in a school yard?" A silly thought, but it is not going to happen to me.

The people who come to us have been chosen by their agencies as qualified and worthy candidates for sniper training. We feel we can entrust them with the skills and knowledge we will pass on, because their agency has done the necessary screening beforehand. That candidate is deemed to be honest, upstanding, emotionally stable and dedicated to serving and protecting the public. Outsiders expect the same level of entrustment simply because they assure us they are good guys.

I'm sorry, but that is not enough. Being an avid shooter, or someone with a keen interest in the art of sniping does not automatically entitle you to unrestricted access to the world of professional snipers. Being a tactical sniper, working as a tactical sniper, involves so much more than marksmanship.

Since this book isn't restricted, I'm sure some of those in question are reading this. And I am sure they are really angry with me by now. Sorry. If they are really serious about wanting to be included, my advice to them is "pay your dues." Go through the process and join a police department. Pass the academy, do your probation, and work your midnight shifts. Earn a spot on the SWAT team. Endure SWAT school and receive the chance to become a sniper. When this ceases to be just a fascination, we'll welcome you with open arms. We'll even show you the handshake.

> "I want no part of a club that would have me as a member."
> —Groucho Marx

BEYOND THE SHOT

Slowly, but surely, the police and sniper community is starting to acknowledge the emotional and psychological impact which can result from the aftermath of life-threatening, traumatic events. Officers involved in deadly force incidents fall into this category. The use of deadly force by a police officer is a unique event in law enforcement. This is even more acute in the role of the police sniper. His actions are usually more intimate and deliberate than other deadly force encounters. As a result, it requires a special level of follow-up. Although these post-shooting steps should be followed in the aftermath of any police shooting, this chapter speaks specifically to the needs of the police sniper.

This chapter is divided into two areas of focus, the first being the responsibilities of agency administrators. This includes the Chief, command staff, supervisors and investigative personnel. The second portion addresses the sniper himself. Both are intended to minimize the potential traumatic effect on the individual officer, as well as the rest of the agency, while insuring an accurate and complete investigation of the incident.

This is built on recommendations from clinical psychologists, attorneys, criminal investigators, and agency administrators. Their collective findings are based on clinical and research data from hundreds of police-involved shootings. It also reflects the first-hand experiences of snipers who have pulled the trigger.

The primary concerns of the agency, following a police sniper shooting, must be the physical and emotional well being of the sniper and all other on-scene police personnel. The preservation and accurate recording of physical evidence is also a vital area of concern, but secondary to the need to determine the health and safety of all persons immediately involved in the incident.

I strongly suggest the following post-shooting procedures in any event involving the use of deadly force by a police sniper:

Check on the health of the sniper. Once the fighting has ended and the physical danger has passed, your first priority must be checking on the welfare of your personnel. If any are injured, then securing medical attention is your very next concern. Plus, expressions of concern for the psychological well being of personnel by the individual in authority has been demonstrated to be of significant value to the long-term welfare of the involved officer. Simply hearing, "Are you okay?" from a superior can work wonders for his emotional recovery.

An additional note here—this well-being check should extend to the sniper's partner as well, even if the partner did not shoot. Interviews with sniper teams have shown sniper shootings have an emotional impact on observers and shooters. Many times, the observer's reactions to the event go unnoticed and as a result, unaddressed.

As soon as it is safe and practical, secure the scene. Ensure that all steps are taken to collect and record accurate crime scene data, as well as account for witnesses. This is a time sensitive issue. Photographic and video evidence needs to be taken as soon as possible to accurately record lighting and weather conditions at the time of the shot. Emphasis should also be placed on recording the sniper's hide position and his field of view.

Allow the sniper (or his partner) to oversee the evidentiary collection of his weapon. This step is contingent upon the sniper's physical and psychological condition, of course. Keeping the sniper involved at this point helps him to retain a level of control over the events unfolding. In the event he is not capable of handling this, another sniper, or a teammate who is familiar with sniper weapons should be given responsibility for this.

Also, make every effort to return the rifle to the sniper as soon as possible. Snipers develop a unique relationship with their rifles, strange though it may seem to outsiders. Getting his gun back to him will be important in the healing process, trust me.

Remove the sniper from the scene as soon as is practical, and require that the officer be examined at a medical facility. There may be no obvious physical injury, but the emotional and mental stress may have a serious impact. Hyperventilation, elevated blood pressure, and other stress-related symptoms have been documented in officers after shootings. This also insulates the sniper from unnecessary questions, and scrutiny from bystanders, other officers and the media.

Advise the sniper on the progression of events from that time forward. The unknown creates fear. Being aware of what is going to happen to him will help the involved officer to relax and deal with the next few days.

Encourage the sniper to contact his family. It is important for him and his family to confirm that he is all right. In this age of instant news, you don't want the media making the notification.

Encourage the sniper to secure legal representation as soon as possible. An attorney with a background in use of force issues should be previously identified and available 24 hours a day. Emphasize to the sniper that there is no allegation of wrongdoing, but this is a highly charged, emotional moment. The sniper needs to have an impartial third party at work to help him deal with procedural issues and decision-making.

Supply the sniper with peer support. The effects of post-traumatic stress can start almost immediately. Peer support is a clinically recognized, therapeutic safeguard. A non-involved teammate would be the best choice.

An individual, psychological debriefing for the sniper should be mandatory. It should be scheduled to occur within the first 72 hours of the incident. This is deemed the optimal time frame for post-crisis intervention. Making it part of the policy removes the stigma of seeing a mental health professional, and is recognized as a vital step in the recovery process for the sniper.

A group debriefing, consisting of all involved individuals (including dispatchers) should also be mandatory. Research has demonstrated that the input from peers who have shared the event with the sniper can be one of the most important aspects of psychological well-being. Such a group debriefing is also a key factor in assessing lessons learned and future training needs.

The sniper should have a mandated administrative leave (not suspension with pay), effective immediately. He should return to work only when he feels emotionally ready to return to duty, but no sooner than three days. Other than the most basic Garrity statement, he should not be forced to give any official statement, written or verbal, until after returning from this diffusing period. The sensory and cognitive distortions caused by his traumatic event may prevent him from giving an accurate account until those effects have subsided.

As soon as is practical, brief the rest of the department about the incident. This incident clarification is intended to educate uninvolved officers. Provide enough information to dispel rumors and minimize destructive second-guessing, but do not compromise any ongoing investigations.

The media should be provided with accurate information regarding the event, taking care not to compromise any ongoing investigations, or the privacy of the involved sniper. In the absence of information provided by your office, media outlets may resort to speculation and unsubstantiated sources for their reports. Many times, those reports have caused unwarranted controversy.

At the conclusion of the investigations, a complete tactical debriefing of the incident should be offered to the entire agency. This is an opportunity to look objectively at lessons learned, and to improve on tactics and planning for next time. Good or bad, there is nothing gained by keeping your agency in the dark about what happened. Lessons shared save lives.

Prior to going back into service, the sniper should be required to re-qualify with his weapon. Re-qualification provides reassurance for the sniper in his skills, his willingness to engage in expected responsibilities, and the readiness of his weapon system. It provides documentation for the agency the sniper maintains the required degree of proficiency with his weapon, and that he is fit to return to duty in his assigned position. This step was recommended by a number of snipers after their shooting events.

For the individual sniper, many of his after-action steps closely parallel those of his agency, with some important differences. The goal of his actions is survival—physical, legal and psychological. If the sniper himself is not in a frame of mind to follow these steps, you, as his partner, should take responsibility for making sure he is properly taken care of.

Take all necessary steps to preserve the crime scene. Freeze the moment until your position, field of view, the conditions at the time of the shot, and all other pertinent information is accurately recorded.

Oversee the collection of your weapon. If possible, handle this step personally. If not, have an arrangement with your partner in place to make sure someone you trust will take responsibility for this. Render the weapon safe. Record scope settings, shooting position and other details. Package the weapon in a padded case for future handling and transport to the crime lab.

Protect your legal rights. Speak to no one outside of your hide until you have consulted your legal representative. You have done nothing wrong, but you need to have an objective professional at the scene looking out for your best interests. Again, this is something to have arranged ahead of time. If your agency or union doesn't provide counsel as a matter of routine, have a private attorney on retainer for this purpose.

Separate yourself from the scene as soon as is practical. In the meantime, watch what you say and to whom. Assume no area is secure from unauthorized ears.

Seek out or accept peer support. (Take care not to discuss the details of the incident in this context. There is no legal privilege of communication with other officers.) Now is not the time for macho heroics. You have been involved in the most traumatic event in police work. The emotional effects can either be dramatic, or insidious. Having friendly support close by can't hurt.

Take full advantage of the cooling off period offered by your agency. Use the time to relax and distance yourself from the event. Don't listen to the news, or read the papers. The stories the media might tell may have no resemblance to the truth. Yelling at the television may not be that therapeutic. Spare yourself the aggravation.

When you are ready, and no sooner, give a formal statement to your investigative bureau regarding the incident. This should be done with the assistance and advice from your legal representative. The statement you give will follow you throughout the life of the investigations that will follow. You want to make sure it is accurate and complete, the first time.

If you feel it is needed for your emotional well-being, seek professional counseling. Continue treatment until you are healthy. Each of us has our own emotional tolerance level. Some individuals will handle an incident such as this with little difficulty. Others will never be the same. It is important to remember, any reaction you have is normal for you. Deal with it in a healthy manner. Your emotional survival is just as important as your physical survival was when the shots were being fired.

Historically, the focus of most sniper training has been on range time. A concerted effort needs to be made from now on to prepare snipers and administrators for what happens after the trigger has been pulled and the gunsmoke has cleared.

LEGEND OF THE PIZZA BOYS

For many years, the snipers on our team have been referred to as "The Pizza Boys." The story behind the name is interesting and sheds light on an important sniper trait.

We were scheduled to go to night training at an off sight. When the training order came out, special emphasis was put on meals. The team leader pointed out the need for every officer to bring a bag lunch, because we wouldn't have time to break away for meals. This wasn't a new practice, but snipers being snipers, we usually found a way to slip out on food runs while the entry grunts pulled out their brown bags and coolers.

When the training day rolled around, we showed up to do our range work. And, as to be expected, the rebels neglected to bring lunches with them. But we pride ourselves on being resourceful. When break time came, the entry team broke out their coolers. The team leader, a guy with no sense of humor, watched us like a hawk. However, much to his surprise, none of us left. Instead, a delivery van from a local pizza place rolled up and out came the delivery guy with a stack of pizzas for—the snipers.

As the aroma of cheese and sausage cuisine filled the room, a legend was born. But there was a lesson to be learned. We proved once again our ability to think outside the box, remain flexible, and solve problems. In the words of Clint Eastwood, we adapted, improvised and overcame.

We're snipers, but we answer to Pizza Boys.

SHOPPING

Buying quality equipment for tactical teams should be a no-brainer. After all, when the team is called out, it is usually a critical incident with lives in the balance. Naturally, the team would want to have equipment its members can count on to be functional and reliable under any conditions. With that in mind, why do so many teams outfit their personnel with junk and try to get by? Quality equipment to do a quality job is not a suggestion, it is the rule. Yet team leaders, administrators and others make purchase decisions based on cost over quality, low bidder over best product.

In this section, I want to look at four major purchases sniper teams will have to make and give some advice to guide your shopping. This is not meant to be a technical primer, but a generic overview of what is currently available. Although I have personal favorites in each category, I will restrain myself and try to maintain the appearance of non-bias.

SNIPER RIFLES

Every sniper needs one. It has to be rugged, reliable and accurate. Once upon a time, your choices were severely limited, but not anymore. There are sniper rifles available to meet every need and price range. However, not all sniper rifles are created equal. Buy a good rifle. Simple advice, but it takes some work to accomplish.

Manufacturers offer rifles in a variety of barrel lengths, tapers and twist rates. Each has pros, cons, and applications. Order that which best suits your shooting needs.

Stocks come in several configurations. Some are adjustable, or offer a range of customization. This is a choice best left up to the individual shooter, since everyone is built a little different, and the gun should fit the shooter. Some like the conventional Monte Carlo style of stock, while many others find the various thumbhole designs more ergonomic and comfortable. One recommendation in choosing a stock is to make sure it is ambidextrous.

Don't buy a rifle based only on a sales pitch or because everyone else is using it. Talk to teams about their experiences with rifles and listen to what they feel are strengths and weaknesses of their systems. Contact local vendors and get rifles to T & E with your shooters. Listen to their feedback; after all, they are going to be the end users.

Durability and ruggedness are factors that must be considered. A sniper rifle is going to be exposed to a fair amount of abuse in the field. The gun has to be able to withstand everything a sniper is going to throw at it and still function reliably. There are guns available with a reputation for their toughness. Conversely, there are great shooting guns that will prove to be too delicate for sniper work.

How serviceable is the gun? Are there parts readily available for it? Are there gunsmiths in the area qualified to work on it? Is it a gun that will have to be sent off to a distant custom shop for routine maintenance, taking the rifle, and possibly the sniper, out of service for extended periods?

A good rifle, well maintained, will outlast several cheaper rifles purchased during the same time frame. In the long run, there is no savings realized by buying a cheap rifle that has to be replaced or refitted every few years. Spec out exactly what you want in a sniper rifle, including accessories, and buy the best rifle you can afford. This is too critical a purchase to trust to the lowest bidder.

Optics

I believe your weapon system is only as good as the scope you put on it. The best sniper rifle in the world is worthless if the scope won't hold a reliable zero. A really good scope is worth its weight in gold, and with a little shopping, won't cost you that much. Like the weapon system, the scope has to be rugged and reliable. All of the abuse your rifle is going to be exposed to in the field and training is going to be shared by the scope. Every round fired in training is going to subject your scope to the repeated slam of recoil. I have seen bad scopes fail in spectacular ways. You don't want something like that in the back of your mind, eating away at your confidence. You want to know you are going to hit what you aim at because you can trust your equipment.

There are more than a few good, sniper-quality scopes on the market. But don't trust magazine ads or catalogs to give you the information you need to make a purchase. Talk to users. Find out what snipers are recommending from their personal experience. They will tell you what holds up and can be counted on. Then, get your hands on samples and try them out yourself and literally see if they are suitable for your application.

Characteristics I would look for in a good tactical scope include:

— Variable power, 3.5 x 14 at a minimum.
— A large objective lens, 50mm is an optimal choice.
— Target turrets with positive click adjustments. ¼ minute clicks are the accepted standard for adjustments.
— Side focus and parallax adjustment.
— Illuminated reticle.
— Heavy-duty tube sealed and weatherproofed.
— High quality glass, which provides a clear and sharp image to the edges of the scope and accurate color transmission.

The best scopes aren't necessarily the most expensive. Do your research and legwork. I can't stress enough how important a good scope is to your performance.

AMMUNITION

This is a case of trying to wean the sniper community off a popular choice, and steering them toward a practical one. The Sierra 168 grain boattail hollow-point was designed to provide a high degree of accuracy when loaded in a match grade configuration. It gained favor with competitive shooters because of its consistent performance. Based on this, tactical shooters have also made it their primary bullet choice.

While there is no question about the accuracy of this type of match grade ammunition, the bullet itself is not a true hollow point, and does not perform as an expanding round. As a result, it has a well-documented history of going through and through human targets. This puts hostages, teammates and other friendly persons near your target at risk. And while snipers should take every possible step to isolate their target in space prior to shooting, sometimes situations limit one's ability to allow for a completely clear impact area. One police shooting in particular illustrated the potential for collateral damage. In that incident, the sniper's round went through the torso of his target, through the door post of his vehicle, through the outer and inner wall of the trailer home behind him, through a kitchen cabinet and the wall of a steel sink, before coming to rest in a pile of clothes in the living room.

For eternity, sniper teams have been buying this round, simply because everyone else buys it. And everyone else buys it because it is accurate. But this round was initially designed to punch holes in paper, not people. It is time to look at alternatives.

Manufacturers of sniper grade ammunition are starting to listen to the concerns of snipers, and several are now offering rounds designed to expand and/or disintegrate after impacting human targets. The aim is to provide match grade accuracy while limiting the probability of over-penetration. As you research your next ammunition purchase, I highly recommend you look long and hard at the new bullets on the market. Collateral damage is one of those unforgivable mistakes in police work. We can and should take steps to prevent this from happening.

Call ammunition manufacturers and tell them you are planning to make your annual ammo purchase. In many cases, they will be happy to send you several boxes to test fire in your guns. Never buy ammunition without testing it. Every gun is different, and every one has a favorite ammunition. Take the time to find out what works best in your guns, then buy enough to train with and use operationally. (I mention buying enough because I have dealt with departments who have tried to get away with buying a case of cheap reloads for practice and a few boxes of "the good stuff" to use on callouts. Doom on you for doing that.) Making the right purchase of the right ammunition may cost your agency a little more money, but the piece of mind and confidence you are buying is priceless.

NIGHT VISION SIGHTS

Night vision sights for sniper teams should not be viewed as an extravagant luxury. Considering the high probability a SWAT call will either begin in darkness, or last into evening hours, night vision capability is a necessity. Not every nighttime callout will necessitate the employment of night optics. Especially in urban environments, there may be enough ambient light to allow for successful operations without night vision. But it is always better to have it in stock and not need it, than the other way around.

There are three types of night vision sighting systems currently in use for sniper rifles. First is the dedicated night sight. This is a night vision scope permanently mounted on a dedicated rifle. The limitations of this application are obvious. Although the cost of these scopes is usually less than most of the day/night systems, you still have to factor in the cost of an additional rifle on which to mount the scope.

A second choice is the day/night system. There are a couple of versions available on the market. One uses a single scope with interchangeable day and night eyepieces. While this is a good concept, historically, the system hasn't had a good track record for reliability. If that changes, this is an option deserving consideration. The other day/night option uses a piggyback system, in which the night vision device mounts on top of the existing riflescope. This system requires adjustments to the riflescope zero settings. It is also heavy and changes the weapon's balance and profile. It is more expensive than most other systems as well. On the positive side, it is rugged, reliable, battle-tested by the military, and provides a high-quality night image.

A third option is the newest offering on the market. This scope mounts in front of the objective lens of the existing riflescope, usually on a special extended rail. This scope is compact, lightweight and does not change the weapon's profile. The system is battle-tested, with the military making use of it with great success in recent field applications. The internal technology is state of the art; the image is clear and sharp. The scope takes full advantage of the existing rifle optics, without zero adjustments. The current cost of this system is comparable to the piggyback style.

Night vision is another item that needs to be shopped for with care. Not all night scopes are created equal. A lot of the low price scopes on the market are either refurbished units, or units using Generation I or II intensifier tubes. Some are surplus units. Don't waste your money. Generation III and above tubes provide the best image quality, which is necessary for accurate target identification, and worth the extra cost. Buy from reputable dealers who will warranty and provide customer support for the products they sell your agency. This is another purchase that should require hands-on demonstrations in your working environment before decisions are made. Some companies will provide this, along with training for your personnel.

Conclusion

As you begin your shopping trip, remember these pointers:

Don't buy anything based solely on a sales pitch, ad or catalog. After all, when was the last time you heard a salesman say, "Our product isn't the best on the market, but you should buy it anyway"? Trust your own research, not their influence.

Don't settle for lowest bidder. Shop with specific specs in mind and buy the best product meeting your requirements. By its very nature, tactical equipment is going to cost more. Be willing to spend more and ready to justify why. Don't compromise your standards.

Don't be afraid to ask for samples or a chance to test products. Vendors will be willing to let their products speak for themselves, if it is a good product. It is important to test items in your working environment, in the hands of your end users. Their feedback should be considered invaluable.

Don't buy based on what you think is a good choice. Consult the end users. In fairness, they will have to use the equipment in the field. They should have input in the purchasing decision making process.

Don't buy a product simply because it is what you have always bought. In the tactical world, things are changing constantly. Better products are out there. Do the homework and test the waters. You want the best products available in the hands of your operators. They deserve nothing less.

THE SITUATION THIS IS

Your team has been called out to handle a hostage situation. Two individuals, we'll call them Nelson and Kelly, were attempting to rob a jewelry store when a passerby spotted them and called the police. The first units arrived before the robbers could leave the store. Seeing the police arriving, Nelson and Kelly retreat into the store and announce they are holding the employees as hostages.

SWAT is called to the scene while negotiators try to reason with the two criminals. They are frightened and agitated. They tell the negotiators five employees are being held in the store at gunpoint. The robbers want to be allowed to leave. Of course, the negotiators tell them surrendering their hostages would be the best step they could take toward a peaceful resolution right now.

SWAT personnel maneuver into position, covering every avenue of escape. Snipers set up and begin to report their observations as they put eyes on the store. They can clearly see Nelson and Kelly holding their frightened hostages at gunpoint in an area between counters.

Negotiations drag on for several hours. Nelson seems to be doing most of the talking on the phone, and he is unyielding in his demand for safe passage from the store. Frustration is edging into his voice as the strain of the standoff is starting to wear on him. He yells into the phone, telling the negotiator he is running out of patience, and if they aren't allowed to escape, they will start killing hostages. This escalation in the threat level is relayed to the command personnel. In turn, they pass the information on to the team. Plans for a possible hostage rescue operation are accelerated.

Suddenly, one of the sniper teams is on the air advising they have Nelson and a female hostage approaching the front door. The door swings open and they stop there in the doorway. All eyes are on the pair as he presses his gun against the hostage's right temple and shouts,

"Give us what we want, or they start dying!" The sniper team is already on him. Two sets of crosshairs quarter his face as two trigger fingers begin to take up the slack on their respective rifles.

The question to you as a sniper is, do you shoot him?

On the face of it, this appears to be a no-brainer. But in the real world we work in, this has been an area of controversy. Discussions on this scenario have been raised during classes and in training scenarios. Some administrators have argued against taking the shot. By killing Nelson, they are afraid Kelly will kill the remaining hostages in retaliation. Several have clearly stated they would never authorize any sniper under their control to take the shot. But what is the alternative? Do we just call his bluff to see how far he will go? Does his action trigger a hostage rescue attempt? Do we allow Nelson to kill a hostage and continue negotiating? How many hostages do we allow him to parade out and shoot under these rules of engagement? How good are you at reading minds?

I have sat in on a number of very heated discussions of these questions. Hopefully, reading this will initiate conversations among your teammates, because this is a situation that needs to be anticipated and planned for ahead of time. You need to know what you are going to do, and why, now. Developing a team philosophy, and possibly a policy, in advance can simplify decision-making in the heat of a critical point in an operation.

I can't, and won't offer the "right" answer to this scenario. What I will offer is my personal feelings. Take them for what they are.

"Control what you can," is the guiding principle. As I sit in my hide, I have no control of the conditions around me. I don't control the weather. I don't control the circumstances that brought me there. I don't control what happens beyond my sight. However, when a hostage taker marches a hostage out into my field of observation and presses a gun to her head, I can control what he will be allowed to do to that hostage. I can control whether that hostage lives or dies at his hands. I control what will happen in that moment in time.

If I shoot Nelson, there is the possibility Kelly will try to kill the other hostages. There is also a possibility he will not. He may take the time to reconsider his position and choose to live and surrender. I don't know which will happen, nor does anyone else. As a result, I can't let my actions be dictated by what might, or might not happen.

I will shoot Nelson, because I can definitely save the life of the hostage he threatens. I control that much. What happens next will have to be dealt with as it happens. I just know I could not stand by and let Nelson, or anyone else kill a hostage in my sight. I will save that hostage because I can.

What would you do? Could you watch and do nothing? Could you look yourself in the mirror the next day, knowing you let a hostage die?

Your job is to save lives.

HOW TO RUIN A SNIPER PROGRAM

There is a segment of the tactical community that seems committed to making it fail. I'm referring to a group of supervisors, administrators and operators set on doing whatever is necessary to ruin their sniper program. In order to make their job easier, and take the guesswork out of the process, I offer this primer. The advice here has been proven to work on ineffective teams around the country.

(A word of caution, though, before I start. A few years ago, I gave a lecture at a conference on this topic. My obvious use of sarcasm and irony in the presentation was lost on one member of the audience. The pained expressions on his face revealed his confusion. Finally, he sheepishly raised his hand and asked, "Are you being serious?" A joke isn't nearly as funny if you have to explain the punchline. Please notice the tongue placed firmly in cheek.)

Start by undermining the foundation of the program. Items like Standard Operating Policies, Mission Statements, training plan and other written policies will only get in the way. Spare yourself the hassle. If you don't have them, no one can hold you accountable to them. This gives you the flexibility to make it up as you go along. Whatever you do is right.

Forget about taking the time to screen sniper candidates. You certainly don't want someone who is motivated and skilled to fill the position. Instead, look to your SWAT team and choose the guy who is too old, fat, or otherwise unable to do entry work, and give him a rifle. After all, snipers just lay down behind a gun and watch while the real team does the real work. Here is a chance to pay off favors, or give the job to a guy who owns a rifle and does a little hunting.

Scrimp on equipment when you can. A penny saved is a penny earned. There is no reason to spend a couple of thousand dollars on a sniper rifle when hunting rifles can be had so much cheaper. Check the evidence locker. You may find a bargain there. The same goes with optics. A scope is a scope. All they do is help you see better. The fancy, high dollar scopes are a luxury purchase. And don't let anyone sell you on the need to spend extra money for match grade ammunition. Match-grade is simply code for "more expensive." If reloaded ammunition, or soft-pointed bullets are good enough for hunting deer, they are good enough for your snipers. After all, how often do they shoot people?

Don't bother to train. Training time takes them away from their real jobs. Sniper schools are a waste of time and money anyway. What do they need to learn? You show up at the call, you get in position; you point your rifle at the bad guy's place. If you see something, you get on the radio. You don't need a week away at some expensive school to learn that. And once they are in service, let them go to the range once in a while to shoot a few rounds, just to make sure the guns work. The fewer rounds they shoot in training, the fewer you have to buy each year. Besides, how often do they shoot people?

If your team gets called out, you have an opportunity to screw up the operation. A good strategy is to make it up as you go. For those of you with a sense of adventure, this is the only way to go. Prior planning prevents poor performance, but why waste time planning for something that might never happen? You're trained police officers. You can handle any problem. When it happens, you'll figure out a solution sooner or later. The use of what might be considered questionable tactics is encouraged at this point. If they work, you get the credit. If they don't, oh well.

Keep a closed mind. Sure there are people and teams who have "been there and done that," but why would you want to listen to them. Just because it worked for them, doesn't mean it will work for you. Besides, you believe in doing it your way. Don't muddy the waters with outside ideas and influences.

Limit their use and discretion. Snipers should never be allowed to stray too far from the pack. It is a tendency of theirs that needs to be curtailed. Exercise strict control over their activities by limiting their discretion, especially when it comes to using deadly force. That is a decision which needs to be made by a person with command level knowledge only. You can avoid the problem by not deploying them at all.

Let the lawyers run the team. Listen to them. Fear of litigation is a good thing. If you don't do anything, you can't get sued for what you do. If you do get sued, admit to nothing, deny everything, blame others, and demand proof.

Don't change anything. Change requires effort. It is easier to stay consistent and stick with what has always worked in the past. "This is the way we've always done it," is a perfectly reasonable rationale for clinging to your old ways.

Gag orders can cover a myriad of sins. If your team does something that might be viewed as controversial or questionable, the last thing you want to do is own up to it. Tell your personnel to shut up and talk to no one. If you don't talk about it, it didn't happen.

It is important to not provide support to your snipers. Since you make the decisions about training, equipment and deployment, it is easy to make sure their requests for more of those items get denied. If they try to go around you to appeal to more sympathetic ears, you are still in a position to torpedo their attempts. They must depend on you for everything, and you don't have to give them anything.

Don't stand behind them in anything they do. This is particularly true if they take a shot on an operation. Distance yourself from their action immediately. If it is determined the sniper did a good job, you can always reappear at his side. If there is any question about his actions, you have deniability.

While we're on the subject of sniper shootings, there is another area of support that needs to be addressed. Post Traumatic Stress is one of those hot catch phrases in the police and tactical community these days. There are those who would have you believe snipers need some sort of emotional support after a shooting. Real cops, real snipers are supposed to be tough enough to handle this. After all, shooting suspects is a part of their job. Don't coddle them. Tell them to act like men and go back to work.

Don't share information with anyone. What happens in your agency stays in your agency. You learned the hard way—why should you make it easy for some one else?

Ignore lessons learned. Information sharing is a two-way communication process. You don't want to share what you learn, and you certainly don't want to be influenced by anything some other team may have learned. After all, just because they did something one way doesn't mean you will handle it the same way, or that the result will be the same. Protect your team from the meddling influence of outsiders.

What will be the end result of your concerted efforts, or lack thereof? Your success in ruining the sniper program will manifest itself in three ways. You will stagnate your program. Wherever it is now in its evolution, it will remain, if not regress. You will discourage your personnel. Some will quit immediately. The more hardcore will try to tough it out, but they will eventually give in as well. No one will ask for extra training time, equipment or work. Ultimately, you will save your agency money, which should make you a local hero. Tens of thousand of dollars that would have been wasted on the aforementioned training and equipment can be allocated to something more useful.

Unbelievable? I have a frightening revelation. As outlandish as some of the statements I just made may have sounded, I didn't have to make any of them up. Snipers, trainers and/or administrators in a variety of contacts around the country made every one of them. There are people in your community who really think like this. The question is why.

Good results reinforce poor practices. Phil Messina said it best. He once wrote, "Sometimes we get medals for being good. Sometimes we get them for being lucky and sometimes we get them for being downright stupid. The problem is when we get medals for being stupid, we encourage others to be as stupid as we were, and they might not also be lucky."

From the days of the first SWAT teams, there have always been stupid people making stupid decisions. Assuming this is not what you have in mind for your sniper team, I hope you are now curious about counteractive courses of action. This can't be allowed to continue just because you have gotten away with it so far.

What to do? Stop whining. So many times I have listened to snipers complain about the state of their teams and programs. They talk about all of the negatives listed here and more. And that's all they do. Whining may make you feel better, but it has never resulted in change.

Instead of complaining, you should get angry. Each of these things compromises your safety and mission effectiveness. People who either don't care, or don't know any better, are putting you at risk. If you passively accept this condition, it will only get worse.

One of the factors paralyzing agencies is fear of lawsuits. In our line of work, every action we take is vulnerable to litigation. Anyone can file a lawsuit about anything. You can't prevent being sued. However, you can avoid losing any lawsuits that are filed against you and your agency. Winning requires preparation in the form of establishing a solid sniper program based on sound principles and established practices and standards. For some agencies, this means changing the way you do things now.

Change requires effort. You can complain all you want about the status quo. Nothing will change until you choose to do whatever is necessary to effect the change. If you want to see improvements in your sniper program overall and in your individual performance, then get to work. Assess the shortcomings in your situation and devise a plan of action. The choices always boil down to make an excuse or make something happen.

I have one last item for you to consider. This is a time for self-assessment. Every jurisdiction needs to have special operations capability. The types of crimes and situations necessitating a SWAT response are non-discriminating when it comes to times and locations. However, not every agency has what it takes to mount a successful SWAT program. Take a hard look at your situation. Does your agency have the manpower, financial resources and the internal commitment to organize and support a functional SWAT program? If you are not willing to do it right, then don't bother to do it at all. To put out a team strictly for show purposes puts people at risk and gives others unrealistic expectations of your ability to protect and save lives. Such teams, and the snipers (and in this case, I use the term loosely) assigned to them are more of a danger than an asset. SWAT requires more than a few dollars, a few hours, and a few good men. This has to be a total commitment on all levels of the agency involved. Do it right, or don't do it at all.

"Nothing of importance will come without effort."
—Dan Wesson

THE MOMENT OF TRUTH

The callout had gone on for what seemed like forever. The sniper had lost track of how long he had been watching the silent drama play out in his scope. A young man, shirtless and covered with tattoos, was holding a middle-aged stranger hostage. The sniper had no idea what their relationship was, or what had brought them to this point. He only knew the young man had a handgun, and he was threatening to kill the woman he was using as a shield unless the police went away. Of course, everyone knew that was not even an option.

The sniper had spent his time watching the hostage taker chain smoke, talk on the phone and wave his gun in a pantomime of menace. As his frustration peaked, he apparently decided to break the stalemate. The young man reached his limits with a violent flourish. Grabbing a handful of hair, he dragged his hostage out of the living room and onto the front porch. The sniper snapped to attention. The hysterical hostage was forced to her knees in front of her captor. The sniper brought his scope to bear on him. The young man raised his gun and pressed it against the back of her head. The sniper did nothing.

Well, not exactly nothing. He got on the radio and advised the rest of the team what was happening. He continued to give a progress report until the first shots rang out. Crimson blossoms sprouted among the tattoos on his bare chest. The young man slumped to the ground as the assault team rushed in to scoop up his hostage and hustle her to safety.

The story is above is fiction, but the situation is not. It is a hypothetical composite built on factual accounts. I am aware of several recent incidents where snipers found themselves in similar circumstances, and when the moment of truth arrived, they did not shoot. This is troubling, but not surprising.

I firmly believe too many snipers are in the trade for the wrong reasons, and with the wrong expectations. They become snipers because it's cool. The "CDI Factor" is high. They get high-speed equipment and special training. They spend time on the line punching holes in paper, and revel in shooting those tight little groups. They are only in this for the range time – target shooters with pagers. They have the insulated attitude that "It will never happen to me." Then, one day, it does. And when it does, they don't know how to react. They never accepted the reality of the job.

In an old western, a gunfighter is asked by a reporter what it took to be successful in his trade. The gunfighter told him, "First, you have to be willing." As police officers, each one of them has been taught shooting fundamentals and the laws regarding using deadly force. Little, if any time has been devoted to conditioning them to being willing. The price police officers have paid in street encounters as a result of this training shortcoming is material for another book. The focus here is the police sniper.

Using deadly force is part of a police sniper's job. However, his application is unique. Unlike an officer on the street, you will generally not be responding in self-defense, shooting as a conditioned reflex. The sniper shot will be a deliberate act of killing. You are going to look your target in the eyes as you stare at him through your scope. You will place your crosshairs on him and press the trigger, dispatching 168 grains of jacketed lead into the cranial vault of your human target. Before the sound fades, you will witness the catastrophic damage your bullet causes, as brains, bone and blood spray in every direction. You will have killed a person.

I want you to understand you are not a target shooter. You are not simply punching holes in paper. Every shot you fire in training is preparation for killing another human being. The problem is, some of you haven't come to grips with this fact.

A training tape making the rounds of late is a dashboard camera video showing a traffic stop in the south. During the course of the stop, the driver and the officer engage in a brief scuffle before the driver breaks away and walks back to his truck. He is then seen on camera retrieving a rifle from behind the seat. He methodically loads a magazine, then loads the weapon, and finally turns to face the officer. What is the officer doing during this time? For over forty seconds, he stands at his car, watching the driver preparing to attack him, while he repeatedly orders him to put the gun down. It's as if he can't bring himself to make the decision to use deadly force first, even if it means saving his own life. If I have heard it once, I have heard it a hundred times, officers say, "I hope I never have to shoot anyone," or "The last thing I want to do is use this gun." For police officers in general, and snipers in particular, deadly force should not be thought of as a last resort. Deadly force is one of a number of force options. It should be used when it is most appropriate to resolve the situation at hand. Trainers have an obligation to make officers understand this. (In a perverse reversal, it almost seems that officers are being conditioned to accept dying as part of their job. By couching it in poetic terms like "making the supreme sacrifice," or "laying down his life," dying in the line of duty becomes a heroic act, rather than losing a life or death encounter.)

In this way, I liken the job of a sniper to a carpenter. He has at his disposal a variety of tools. In doing his job, he will encounter various tasks which can be best accomplished with the most appropriate tool. Cutting a board requires the use of a saw. Driving a nail is best done with a hammer. A police sniper has a variety of tools at his disposal as well. His rifle is just one of those tools, no different from his binoculars or his radio. He just needs to understand there is a time when it will be the most appropriate tool to use to accomplish an end.

The courts recognize the nature of physical conflict and allow police officers to use "appropriate and necessary force" in order to effect an arrest or resolve a confrontation as quickly as possible. Trainers need to encourage this level of response. Officers, regardless of their assignment, must be willing to use it.

Being a police sniper means you may have to kill someone. It will be in defense of a hostage, teammate, or yourself, but you will have to take a life to save a life. Before you spend another minute as a "sniper," you have to honestly answer a question; can you, will you, kill another human being? Only you know the truthful answer to this question, but you owe it to yourself, your teammates, and the public you are supposed to protect, to be honest. You have to know with certainty that if faced with a deadly force situation, you will pull the trigger. "I think I will," or "I won't know until the time comes," are totally unacceptable answers. Staring at the crosshairs, with lives literally hanging in the balance, is not the time to find out you can't do it.

Snipers need to be comfortable with this part of their responsibilities. This is not to suggest you should enjoy killing. However, having to use deadly force is an ugly reality in police work. Sometimes, though, due to the circumstances of the moment, it is the most appropriate course of action to resolve the situation. Respect the sanctity of life, but understand your function as part of the SWAT team, and your authority to take lives to save lives.

The next time you pass a mirror, there is something I want you to do. Go to that place where you are totally honest with yourself. Look into the eyes of the person staring back at you and without flinching, ask him, "Are you willing?" Listen to his answer.

ORLANDO

The following chapter contains controversial information about a very sensitive incident. The information related here is drawn from investigative reports, transcripts, interviews of key involved parties, and personal knowledge. There are those who will not agree with the conclusions drawn here, but the facts will be allowed to speak for themselves.

SYNOPSIS

On July 23, 2000, a sniper killed a hostage. However, the truth behind what really happened that day, and what caused it, is not stated so simply. This is a story of mistrust, misinformation and misplaced blame. The lessons learned on that day should have sent ripples throughout the sniper community. But like so many tactical incidents, the truth is not known nearly wide enough. Hopefully, this will be a chance to change that.

The day before, in South Florida, Jamie Petron committed an armed robbery at a neighborhood convenience store. During the robbery, one clerk was shot and killed, another severely wounded. After he escaped the scene, a statewide alert was broadcast for Petron.

Hours later, an Orange County Sheriff's deputy spotted the wanted vehicle and attempted a felony stop. The stop turned violent immediately, with Petron and the deputy exchanging gunfire. The deputy was wounded and Petron ran from the scene and into a house on the street, which just happened to have an open garage door. At the time, he was seen wearing a green shirt with stripes or designs and shorts. Inside, he immediately began taking hostages to prevent his apprehension. Fired a shot at, and slightly wounded Nequan West. The homeowner, Thelma Mills, also managed to escape. Left behind were Andrea Hall, 16-year-old Althea Mills, 8-year-old Nicholas Hall, and two infants. After Petron took control of the residence, the Orange County Sheriff's Office SWAT team responded to the scene and secured the area.

Negotiations were initiated, but progress was slow. About eight hours into the standoff, Petron exited the interior garage door and fired one round at the OCSO SWAT team. A sniper on scene responded by firing a shot, but missed Petron. This exchange of gunfire resulted in the door being designated the "hot door" for the duration of the incident. This would become significant later.

Negotiations resumed and continued through the night. OCSO was content to wait on Petron as long as he was willing to talk and not harm any of his hostages.

During the morning hours of July 23, Orange County command staff contacted the commander of Orlando's SWAT team to request relief personnel. Orlando's team was subsequently dispatched. Sniper Team #1 was assigned the position covering the "hot door." They set up approximately 77 yards from the interior garage door. The overhead door was about a quarter of the way down, which limited visibility inside the garage.

At approximately 1135 hours, the sniper observed a person exiting the interior garage door. Believing this to be the hostage taker, Jamie Petron, the sniper fired one round from his rifle. The sniper conveyed to his partner his belief he had struck the individual. The partner took over the rifle position and utilized his optics, but could not see any evidence to verify a hit.

A short time later, Petron contacted the negotiators and advised them a hostage had been struck and killed by the round fired.

At 1500 hours, he released the eight-year-old hostage, as well as one of the infants. Negotiations continued through the night.

The following morning, the OCSO SWAT team sent a robot into the house. Petron fired two shots at it, but not before it was able to identify a larger object covered with blankets on the kitchen floor, just inside the garage door.

At some point in time, Petron went into a bedroom and killed himself with a single gunshot to his chest. Later, OCSO SWAT personnel entered the home and recovered the two remaining hostages alive and well. The standoff had lasted fifty-one hours.

REACTION

The standoff in Orlando was big news on all of the media outlets in South Florida. Each day, every newscast led with updates on "this breaking story." When the incident ended with deaths, the feeding frenzy began in earnest.

When I heard a hostage had been killed during the incident, and it hadn't been determined how she had died, my first thought was, "I hope she wasn't killed by a SWAT officer." Later in the day, it was reported she had been killed by SWAT, and I thought, "I hope it wasn't a sniper." The next day, the news came out a sniper's bullet had killed Andrea Hall. I told the person I was with at the time, "I hope it isn't someone I know." It wasn't to be.

The sniper who had fired the shot was someone I knew very well. He was a former student and a friend. I felt horrible. He was living the sniper's ultimate nightmare—he had killed a hostage.

Everywhere, the incident was being discussed. And in most venues, the sniper was being criticized for making a bad shot. I expected it from the media. I was disappointed to see it from members of the tactical community. I had hoped they would be sensitive to the need to wait for the facts and to resist the urge to jump to conclusions based on media reports. Knowing the character and competency of the sniper involved, I knew what had occurred couldn't be as simple as bad target identification. My advice to everyone I talked to in those first few hours was to wait for the rest of the story.

I talked to the sniper a little later. Our conversation helped to clarify a lot of the ambiguous details in the news stories. It also gave me a chance to offer my unqualified support to a sniper and a friend. It would take months, but the truth of the incident slowly came out. Lessons were learned, and hopefully SWAT teams will take heed and never repeat the mistakes that led to this tragedy.

THE SNIPER'S VIEW

The sniper and his partner showed up at the command post after being called out to relieve Orange County SWAT personnel on an overnight callout. They were given a briefing, which included information about the events leading up to the standoff. They were told Petron was holding a black family hostage. He was described as the only white person in the residence. He was 5'8", about 250 pounds, and was last seen wearing a green shirt with possible white stripes or a design, and shorts. No detail was given in describing the family other than they were black. They were also told use of deadly force against Petron was already justified. When they were deployed, it was with authorization to use deadly force to stop Petron at first opportunity.

The sniper and his partner set up across the street from the target location, relieving an OCSO team. Their position was about 77 yards from the interior garage door. A second sniper team was set up in a position that gave them a view of the front door of the residence.

The sniper's partner was on the rifle first, and his thirty-minute watch passed without incident. The sniper took over and his partner stood to stretch, out of sight of the house. The snipers from Team 2 were heard on the radio, advising they saw a heavy set black female at the front door of the house. Within seconds of that announcement, the sniper saw the interior garage door swing open. He alerted his partner to the movement. He then saw a white arm slowly stretch out toward the door handle. As the person leaned out farther, he was able to see the profile of a white face, which was partially concealed by a towel draped over the hair. He waited and watched as he saw the subject was wearing a green shirt with white stripes and white shorts. The person appeared to be heavy set in stature. Since all of these features matched the description his team had been given, and since Petron was the only white person inside the house, the sniper fired on what he identified as his target. The individual fell backwards into the house and out of the sniper's view, but he was confident he had hit him.

His partner immediately took over their position and the sniper was removed, fully believing he had shot Petron. He was devastated to hear shortly afterwards he had instead killed one of the hostages he had intended to save.

THE DEVIL IN THE DETAILS

A series of missteps led up to the unnecessary death of an innocent person. Finger pointing aside, the investigation revealed breakdowns in communications and the assumptions created by them corrupted the decision making process and led to a faulty target identification.

According to all of the Orlando SWAT personnel interviewed, during their briefing, they were told Jamie Petron was a very violent and dangerous individual. He was the only white person in the house, and was described as 5'8", approximately 250 pounds. He was said to be wearing a green shirt and white shorts or pants. The only information they were given about the hostages was that they were a black family. There was supposed to be an adult female, a teenage female, and several small children.

What they weren't told was the family members were very light-skinned. No one was made aware that Andrea Hall was about 5'6" and 260 pounds. No clothing descriptions for the hostages were provided.

Prior to Orlando's team coming in for relief, arrangements had been made with Petron to deliver donuts and juice to the front door of the house. The delivery was made using a robot. Petron told the negotiators he would be sending Hall out at some point to retrieve the food. According to their testimonies, this information was not passed on to the team. An Orlando liaison officer was in the command post with OCSO negotiators, but no one there advised him.

Because of poor communications, the wheels of disaster were set in motion. It is unclear who was the person the sniper team saw at the front door, but seeing her established her position in the minds of the teams. When the garage door swung open, the sniper alerted to the movement. As the person appeared at the door, the sniper made a split second target assessment. Based on the information he had available to him at that moment, the person he saw in his scope matched the description of Jamie Petron. Acting on what he determined to be positive target identification, the sniper fired a shot. The flaw in the process was the reliability of the description. If the personnel on the scene at that time were told about the similar physical characteristics of Petron and Hall, I am sure it would have slowed their reaction times in order to further facilitate a positive identification. I am also sure knowing they may see a hostage appear at one of the doors to pick up food would have figured into their decision making process as well.

IN THE AFTERMATH

The sniper spent nearly six months at home on administrative leave while the various investigations ran their course. In the meantime, the sniper community and the media were in full frenzy mode. Everyone had theories and opinions about what happened, most without the benefit of any factual information.

Because I had trained the sniper, I started receiving phone calls from media outlets as soon as the sniper's personnel file was made available to them. As is our practice with media inquiries, we told them nothing more than the sniper was a good student and a good person. We provided no details about the content of his training or his performance while in school.

When Internal Affairs called, they wanted details. I supplied them with a copy of the course outline for their scrutiny. I answered a number of questions over the phone and I sat through a two-hour interview with an investigator. One of the important issues we discussed was the emphasis on what we categorize as the Target Engagement Sequence. It is a five-step process we teach every sniper to follow before every shot. The five steps are Acquire, Identify, Isolate, Engage, and Evaluate. I explained each step to him in great detail, and we spent extra time on the Identify step. In question was what did we feel was necessary for a proper target identification. In law enforcement sniping, nothing less than a positive facial identification is acceptable. However, the accuracy of that identification depends on the reliability and quality of the information provided to the sniper at the time. I was given a hypothetical situation (which in retrospect was very similar to this incident) and asked what type of information would the sniper act upon. I told him, seeing a white face, even in profile, plus matching physical and clothing descriptions, could provide enough information to make an accurate identification. The sniper would be the final judge in determining the threshold of certainty in making a facial ID. This is especially true if you have been told your bad guy is white and all other involved parties are black. However, if the sniper is told his bad guy is a dark-skinned white male, and his hostages are fair-skinned blacks, that factor alone would require the sniper to be far more cautious in making an identification, raising the threshold of certainty even higher.

In this case, one of the primary lessons that have to be learned is the importance of sharing all available information with all involved tactical elements, in a timely manner. How a sniper interprets what he sees is directly influenced by what he knows at the time. Making sure everyone had detailed descriptions and current information about anticipated actions by hostages and bad guys is not optional. There was no tactical advantage gained by limiting the amount of information given out at the briefing when OPD personnel took over the scene. I don't know if it was a conscious decision to withhold information or if it was just a series of unfortunate oversights. In either case, the end result was the same.

The sniper received great support from friends and strangers during his ordeal. Phone calls, emails and letters came in from all over the country, rallying behind a police officer enduring a tragic event. Several teammates stood by him in a big way. However, within his own agency, he dealt with alienation and isolation from other officers and teammates. He recounted instances where people would see him coming down a hall in the station and they would go the other way, or pretend they were suddenly busy, just to avoid having to speak to him. At a time like this, an officer would like to know he has at the very least, tacit support from those in his agency.

His actions that day were scrutinized and debated by the media. Writers of articles and editorials took both sides, some supporting an officer in a tough situation, some attacking him and police use of force in general. One editorial piece accused the sniper of making a bad decision, and performing poorly under stress. Ordinarily, this is to be expected in police shootings. However, the author of the piece was the sniper's chief, speaking out shortly after the civil decisions had been released. An eyebrow raiser, at the very least.

Ultimately, the State's Attorney's office ruled the shooting was not criminal and closed their investigation. The agency closed their internal investigation without substantiating any charges against the sniper. The city and the county negotiated an out of court settlement with the family of Andrea Hall.

After hanging in limbo for nearly half a year, the sniper found out he had been exonerated. He eagerly returned to work, expecting to pick up where he left off. Instead, he was greeted with the news he had been relieved of his SWAT position, and reassigned from his plainclothes detail to a more discrete location. He was being buried, but the team player quietly accepted his new post and has made the most of it.

The sniper has taken full responsibility for his actions that day. He firmly, and rightly, believes he did what he was trained to do. He acted on the information he had available to him at that moment, identified his target, and took his shot, when the intention of saving the lives of others. He did not accidentally shoot a hostage. He deliberately shot what he identified, based on what he knew at that time, as Jamie Petron. To his credit, he has said, given the same set of circumstances tomorrow, he would make the same decision. That's how sure he was of his identification. That level of certainty has helped him deal with the incident's aftermath.

Another important element in his emotional survival was the strength of his faith. The topic of religion is a touchy one with tactical officers, but belief in God can be a great comfort in times of turmoil and uncertainty.

What happened in Orlando over those fifty-one hours sent out ripples locally and throughout the tactical community, which still haven't subsided. Changes were made in policies and procedures, teams were reconfigured, and lives have been altered forever. There is more to the story, which would best be told from the perspective of the sniper himself, and because I am going to encourage him to write it, I don't want to steal his thunder. I just hope the lessons learned in Orlando aren't wasted; otherwise Andrea Hall's death was in vain. We can't change the past, but we can control the future.

> "Also I heard the voice of the Lord saying,
> whom shall I send and who will go for us.
> Then said I, here am I, send me." — Isaiah 6:8

CHOOSING A SNIPER SCHOOL

As important as it is for snipers to receive training, it is equally important to make wise choices in obtaining that training. Training time and dollars are at a premium for most police agencies. Care must be taken in choosing schools to which to send your snipers. Otherwise, it is very easy to throw away valuable time and money. Here is some help in making your decision.

Cost alone is not a good barometer for the quality of the school. More expensive doesn't automatically mean better. In fact, many of the higher priced schools around the nation are overrated, to be polite. Salaries, travel expenses, and high overheads can drive up the costs to the students. Conversely, a low price is not a reliable reflection of the quality of instruction provided by the school. Many inexpensive and free schools provided by agency training units and small companies have great reputations and track records. This due in part, I believe, to the fact some of the best sniper instructors in the field teach because they love the art, not because they are getting paid.

Do not allow yourself to be overly impressed by a slick website, fancy catalog or grandiose claims. Advertising is meant to generate business. There is no obligation, legal, moral or otherwise to honestly portray the product. Look beneath the covers and read between the lines. No school can teach everything there is to know about sniping. Run like crazy from any school or instructor that claims otherwise. Claims to be the "best, finest or leading," are easy to make and impossible to quantify. They should not influence your decisions.

Check out the instructors. Once upon a time, there were only a handful of resources available for police snipers to seek out training. In the last decade, catering to the sniper community has become a growth industry. New schools and new instructors are springing up almost daily. However, not everyone putting on a class has the qualifications to do so. Ask the instructors for their credentials. Find out what experience they have, as operational snipers as well as instructors. Are they still active in the field, or are they long retired and teaching what they used to do once upon a time? You'd be surprised at the number of instructors working in some schools who have never worked as a sniper, either law enforcement or military. I wonder how one can effectively teach a discipline you have never done yourself? How much credibility does an instructor with no operational experience to draw upon really have? Even more heinous are the individuals who claim credentials and accomplishments that are blatantly false. A little research can go a long way here. I would be leery of an instructor who seeks to impress by regaling students with war stories of past exploits. I would be equally afraid of an instructor who shies away from talking about his past, because his missions are "still classified."

Find out what the school teaches. Are their tactics, techniques and philosophies based on reason and sound logic? Is it a trigger school, with the bulk of the course spent on the range, or is it a well-rounded sniper education? Is equal weight given to classroom instruction, fieldcraft skills, and marksmanship? Do the instructors emphasize teaching students their trade? Some schools take great pride in being a physical gut check, and feel that failing a percentage of each class reinforces how tough their school is. I personally feel the job of an instructor is to instruct. If a student fails, isn't that a reflection of the job done by the instructor?

Find out who the school teaches. A number of schools are open to law enforcement, military and "qualified civilians." If they open their classes to civilians, you will have to make a decision as to whether or not you want your personnel to attend. This issue has caused us more than a few debates over the years. While I recognize there are civilian shooters with more skill and rifle time than I will ever achieve, there is a time and place for us to mingle and share knowledge. A police sniper school is not it. This is not meant to be a fantasy camp. This should be a place of police (or military) oriented training, where sensitive information can be openly discussed. Tactics and operational issues don't need to be taught to people outside of the community. Civilians wouldn't be tolerated in a class of motor officers, or a street survival course. Why should a different level of privacy be expected for sniper school?

This is usually a financial issue for the school in question.

What is the course content? A good school will be happy to share with you an overview of the course curriculum. There should be a balance in the instruction offered. The topics should address the operational needs of your snipers. Spending a day on the range, shooting 600-yard bullseyes is a fun confidence builder, but is it done at the expense of more practical shooting exercises? Shooting in different environments is important, but so are legal issues, report writing, and observation skills. In my experience, many students report disappointment with schools they have attended because they didn't meet their educational expectations. Have some idea what your snipers need to learn and find schools that will meet those needs.

The longevity and stability of the school should also be an issue of concern. How long has the school been in business? What is the turn over rate among the instructor staff? These things become important in the future. If one of your snipers is involved in a shooting, training records and content may be examined. There may also be a need to have instructors provide depositions or court testimony in criminal or civil hearings. Will they be around two, three, five years from now? Have they been available for that type of support in the past?

Do they have a good safety record? Some schools have been guilty of dangerous exercises and practices, which place their students at risk. Any school that would allow this should be avoided like the plague.

Don't be afraid to ask for references. Any reputable school or instructor will be happy to have you contact former students for honest opinions. Follow up by talking to those students. Cops can be brutally honest in their assessments of training and trainers. Given the opportunity, they will be able to tell you whether the school and its instructors were good or bad, and why.

Do your homework. This is important enough to merit the effort. You want your snipers to receive the highest quality of instruction, from the most qualified instructors, for the best price. Remember, this is about more than just time and money. The desired end product is a well-trained, operationally ready sniper.

.

A SHORT STORY

I have found that people are fascinated by snipers. They are also a little frightened of us. There is definitely a mystique that surrounds snipers. A lot of it is fed by the media's portrayal of us. To many of them, we are silent, soulless, stone killers.

Once, I was sitting around the office with a number of officers that I worked with at the time. Killing time, the conversation wandered from topic to topic, before settling on someone's curiosity about the sniper position.

One officer had occasionally alluded to his belief that snipers are killers without a conscience. I explained to him and the others we weren't cold-blooded assassins, but there had to be a certain level of emotional detachment involved in order for us to perform our job. This meant depersonalizing every callout and thinking in terms of mission goals and priority of lives. This apparently disturbed one of the listeners. He said, "We have worked together since the academy. You mean to tell me, that if I took hostages and they called you out, you could shoot me?" Without hesitation, I turned and looked him in the eye and said, "John, when the pager goes off, you are just another target." The color left his face. The atmosphere in the room became so thick you could cut it with a knife. But in that moment of awkward silence, I knew everyone in the room understood the single-minded focus this professional sniper brought to his trade.

In stark counterpoint, there is another side of the equation. Teammates and hostages are people, with parents and children, spouses and friends who care about them. I never lose sight of my responsibility to protect the lives of those who matter.

I have a job to do. My desire is to do it very well. I am not a dangerous person. I don't want to be feared. Just understand the people who chose to do this, and respect their ability.

"Some who live deserve to die. Some who die deserve life. Do not take lightly the power of death and judgment you wield. Feel the weight of its finality."

—American Indian Proverb

SETTING PRIORITIES

Perhaps I expect too much. Or maybe, I have my sights set on an unrealistic goal. But, several times in the space of a few weeks, I was disappointed by snipers who didn't share my commitment to the art. I just don't know if the fault was theirs or mine.

The first was a conversation with a sniper who called the office one afternoon, looking for information on a training issue. During the course of our discussion, I invited him to attend one of several upcoming sniper training events and competitions. I emphasized the chance to get good training and spend quality time in the company of snipers. He surprised me by telling me, "I'd love to, but I want to go hunting this fall. You got to set your priorities." I thought saving lives was a priority.

The second incident came a few days later, during a lecture. I talked at length with the class about being willing to go the extra mile to prepare yourself for your mission. This could mean being willing to spend your own time and money to get the equipment and training you need, especially if your agency can't or won't support you. Again I was surprised, and disappointed, when one of the students confessed, "That might be okay for you, but I have a family, and kids. I would rather spend my time with them. And my money, too."

The third came from an agency requesting information about the ASA Certification Program. After exchanging a few e-mails to answer a series of questions, their final reply stated, "We don't want to go through the process unless we can preview the written test and have a chance to shoot the qualification course before we apply." They didn't want to pay the application fee unless they were assured they could pass. Grrrrrrr!

I understand the importance of spending quality time with the family. I understand the limits of the disposable income some people have to spend. I also understand the ego involved in wanting to always do well in front of your peers. What I don't understand is when we lost sight of our mission.

Someone once taught me, "The chief duty of every sniper is to master his craft." You have taken on a job with huge responsibilities. Each callout, you literally are dealing in life and death. With such high stakes, you need to be willing to do whatever is necessary to allow you to master your craft. To me, this means setting aside time to train on my own, because the time I get officially is not enough. It means spending my own money to purchase the little extras my agency won't provide. It means training to be able to do my job really well, because that is what is expected and required of me, not just because I want to be able to pass the next qualification course.

Perhaps, I can make the point more personal. A loved one of yours is taken hostage in my city, your spouse, or your child. My SWAT team is called out and deployed. You are there in the crowd, waiting and watching our every action. As we go about our business, you have a level of expectation in regards to my competency as a sniper. Nothing less than a life-saving performance will be satisfactory. If I fail, what excuse can I make to you and your family that will mitigate your loss? What can I say to make not being ready to do my job acceptable to you? Am I wrong to hold you to the same standard and level of personal responsibility?

I have said it before on many occasions, but it bears repeating here. In the real world we work in, no one will care about how little support you get from your agency. No one will care whether you get ample training time and money for equipment. They could care less about your personal situation or your home life. It won't matter that you were tired, sleepy, hungry, cold or just not ready. The only thing that will matter to your team, the media, the public and that concerned loved one standing in the crowd, is whether you were able to do your job. The standard you will be judged by is perfection on demand. To you, this should mean deciding what really is important and setting priorities.

> "The will to win compares little with the will to prepare
> to win." —Paul "Bear" Bryant.

HOW TO BE A BETTER SNIPER

Welcome to the How-To portion of the book. I won't be giving away any trade secrets, but I want to share some personal beliefs. These are hints and lessons I have picked up over the years. Although, keeping with the theme, these how-to hints may be a little off the mainstream.

Remember, this is not science. Things like ballistics, ranging formulas and bullet drop charts are subject to the rules of science. But beyond that, much of sniping is an art. Success as a sniper depends on you finding the best combination of weapon, optics, ammunition, training, tactics and style, and then making that package your own. This can't, and shouldn't be taught or dictated to you. You should seek advice from other knowledgeable snipers and tap into their pool of operational experience. Everything else you will learn by trial and error. Put together elements that will make you the best sniper you can be. Make this art your own. Don't settle on being a cookie cutter sniper.

Learn to write. Your primary role as a sniper is to observe and report. Much training goes into teaching you to observe (KIMS games). Very little emphasis is given to reporting. Snipers have to be good communicators. Information is useless if it can't be passed on in clear and concise language. In the real-time world of a tactical operation, information is absolutely vital. Your ability to paint a picture with words will help team members, negotiators and command staff plan and execute a safe resolution to your critical incident.

In the aftermath of a sniper shooting, the sniper may be called on to write an after-action report, or give a statement. He may also have to testify in criminal, civil and internal investigations. Because of the importance and longevity of your reports, they must be correct. I tell students their report, whether written or verbal, must be colorful and compelling prose. You must possess the ability to paint a picture with words that transports your listener to your side, your partner in that sniper hide. He must be made to see what you saw, think what you thought, and ultimately, do what you did. Anything less is not a good enough report.

Most people aren't born great communicators. Becoming one means taking the time and making the effort to add this to your training schedule. Taking a class in creative writing or public speaking should be considered sniper training.

Learn to see. Remembering your primary role, it is hard to report what you don't see. Effective snipers need to learn to see the world in detail. Years of inattention have worked to make us visually lazy. As a result, most people see only the obvious or things they are looking for. They do not take the time to see what they are looking at. One of my favorite training tapes is a news clip about a woman who was stabbed in the back in a random attack. The woman wasn't sure what hit her, but since she didn't feel any real pain, dismissed the incident and went about her business. She walked down a main street to visit a recycling center, and then went to the local grocery store to do her shopping, before heading home. It wasn't until she reached her house did she discover the handle of a large knife was sticking out of her back. Amazingly, she had been in the presence of people all morning, and no one had taken notice of the knife in her back or the blood on her coat. We put on blinders and see only what we expect or are looking for. The rest of the world is an easily forgotten blur.

Be willing to admit you don't know everything yet. The training of a sniper is a journey, not a destination. No school, book, videotape or instructor can teach you everything there is to know about the art of sniping. Each of these can provide a piece of an educational mosaic. Every sniper, if he wishes to be successful, has to be an insatiable student of his art. Go to as many schools, seminars and competitions as you can. Read every article and book you can get your hands on. Go online and research what is happening in the sniper world, including equipment, training and callouts. Join professional associations and network with others in your trade. Learn everything you can and share what you have learned.

Don't be afraid to fail in training. I find that snipers like to go to the range, get comfortable, then spend the day shooting little three-round groups. They pat themselves on the back and go away thinking they have accomplished a day of good training. But, what do you learn by repeatedly doing something you already do well?

Growing requires reaching. Athletes get bigger, faster and stronger by pushing physical limits and in the process stimulating their bodies to adapt. In order to grow as a sniper, you must be willing to push your limits and test yourself. This means you have to try things you don't do well. Therefore, training time needs to be spent partly on reinforcing learned skills, then working on your weaknesses. If positional shooting is something you don't do particularly well, the only way to get better is to practice it. Your groups won't be worth bragging about at the start, but improvement will come with quality practice time. Whether your weaknesses are night shooting, stress shooting, weak shoulder shooting, movement skills, or whatever, spend time failing in training learning to do each of these things better. As someone once said, if you always do what you've always done, you will always get what you already have.

Get into better shape. On most callouts, snipers will have to deploy to a remote location to set up their hide. You will have to carry your rifle, ammunition, and additional equipment as you walk, run, climb and crawl into position. After executing that stalk, your real job has just begun. You will now be expected to perform your primary job, staying alert and tuned into everything going on at the crisis site for the duration of the callout. Whether the callout lasts ten minutes or ten hours, you are expected to be at your best throughout. After ten hours, you may be called upon to overcome fatigue and execute a perfect shot. The ability to perform physically and mentally at peak levels for extended periods requires superior conditioning. The ability to drive your body and mind the extra mile that is sometimes necessary comes from a lifestyle of discipline, consistent with a person committed to a fitness program.

The importance of physical fitness to performance in the tactical environment can be summed up in a quote by one of my favorite football coaches. Vince Lombardi motivated his players in training camps by reminding them, "Fatigue makes cowards of us all." When you are running that last mile of the day, and your legs have turned to lead, remember this admonition, "You can't fake endurance."

Visualization is the next best thing to being there. There is great power in the use of visualization as a training tool. This has been proven in a number of scientific settings, as well as in field applications. Snipers should take advantage of this. Visualization allows you to practice every facet of your job. You can put yourself through a stalk and learn to overcome the variety of obstacles you may encounter. You can be on the range, going through the fundamentals of firing each and every shot.

Crisis rehearsal gives you opportunities to vicariously respond to countless scenarios. Using visualization, you can plan a mission, throw in variables, and work through contingencies, all from the comfort of your living room. Make use of your imagination and gain callout experience.

Never miss a putt in your mind. I know this one confused you. Tiger Woods was once asked about the secrets to his success as a golfer. His answer was all about self-confidence and belief in his abilities. "I never missed a putt in my mind." The philosophy wasn't lost on me. Time, practice and dedication will give you the physical skills you need to be a good sniper. Those physical skills need to rest on a foundation of unwavering confidence. You have to believe there is no shot you can't make. You have to believe there is no situation you can't handle. Your attitude has to border on cockiness. But understand cockiness is confidence built on a foundation of skills. If you have physically prepared yourself in training, the rest is mental. In your visualizations, never miss a shot in your mind. Never doubt your ability to do whatever is necessary to succeed. Always tell yourself, "I can make this shot." Because the first time you say you can't, you won't.

Know the rules. Since part of your job may involve using deadly force, it is important you know with certainty when you can employ it. Study your state statutes and departmental policies regarding use of force. Discuss your team's rules of engagement with your teammates and team leaders. Get answers to all of your questions ahead of time. There is no time on an operation to seek clarification. Be able to act decisively in all situations, confident your actions are legally and morally justified.

Train for the task, not just the test. Your effectiveness as a sniper will not be judged on how well you shoot qualification course. Still, many snipers make passing the qualification course the focus of their training programs. If they can make an accurate cold shot at 100 yards, and follow that up with a reasonable three round group, they are satisfied with their abilities. Their training revolves around shooting well enough to pass a qualification course, or win a competition. However, when the pager goes off, your ability to make a static cold shot with no stress is not what your job will require. Training has to prepare you for the reality of your job. Any set of circumstances you can dream up, or that have occurred in other operations need to be addressed in training. Your job as a sniper requires you to learn and master a wide spectrum of skills. Don't be satisfied knowing just enough to earn a certificate or pass a test. This is so much more than just punching holes in paper.

Learn to do it right first. I watch snipers in class and competitions as they struggle to load their weapons, or fight with their bolt during a stress course. They become so engrossed in trying to do simple things fast, sometimes they can't do them at all. Take the time to learn how to do things correctly. Practice makes permanent. Repetition of a skill builds muscle memory. However, your muscles don't know the difference between good technique and bad. Practice them correctly over and over, in slow motion if necessary, until they become second nature. Familiarity with a technique will help you develop an economy of motion. Speed comes from doing it correctly, quickly, with the least wasted effort. Little things do matter.

Know why. So much of what snipers are taught has been passed down and simply accepted at face value. You need to be inquisitive. Everything you do, from training to operational issues, should be done for a good reason, and you should know what it is. I remember a beer ad campaign from a few years ago in which the tag line was, "Why ask why?" While the consumers they were appealing to may be willing to be lemmings, you can't and shouldn't. Ask why, and in the absence of ready answers, do the research and find out why. Searching leads to discovery. If the reason doesn't make sense, then stop doing it and find a better, more practical way along with a rational reason to do it.

Make sniping your passion. Because mastering this art requires so much time and practice, it has to be something you really love to do. Why did you become a sniper? Is it because you want to save lives, or to feed your ego? Is this a personal challenge to you or are you simply fascinated by the toys? Over the years, I have met too many people who became snipers for the wrong reasons. The job of a sniper is all about saving lives. To do it well, requires dedication, desire and passion.

To become a good sniper, you have to love the work and the discipline. Training has to be something you want to do, not something you feel you have to do. Your position as a sniper is important. Lives depend on your abilities. This art deserves your total devotion and nothing less.

Buy good equipment. This seems like a no-brainer, but you'd be surprised how many sniper teams to this day violate the basic tenets of equipment. You need quality equipment to do a quality job. This means you will have to spend money. By its very nature, tactical equipment is going to be more expensive. Don't try to cut corners by trying to suffice with surplus gear, or hand me down equipment. I can relate too many horror stories about equipment failing at critical times in operations. Cheap equipment is cheap for a reason. Is saving a few dollars now worth the lives of your teammates?

Do, or do not. Admittedly, my inspirations come from strange places. Long ago, in galaxy far, far away, Luke Skywalker told Yoda he would "try" to complete a certain task. Yoda told him very seriously, "Do, or do not. There is no try." His comment to a Jedi Knight in training applies to you as a sniper as well. When the pager goes off and you respond, lives are at risk. People around you expect you to do a job. Your preparation and mindset have to be geared to accomplishing that end. No one will care about your lack of support, training or sleep. No excuse for coming up short will be acceptable. Your performance will be measured by whether you succeeded or failed. Do, or do not. There is no try.

The problem is what the problem is. Everyone has heard the proverb about accepting what you can't change. This is another version of that sentiment. When a callout occurs, you can't control or influence the time, place or circumstances. Don't allow yourself to be distracted by those things. It is pointless wasting brainpower worrying about things you can't change. Deal with the situation as it is laid out for you. Focus on solving the problems presented by the callout and prevailing.

Train as if lives depended on it.

MEDIA RELATIONS

Law enforcement has always had a tumultuous relationship with the media. The roots can be found in the mistrust created by a history of inaccurate reporting and unscrupulous tactics. But in this day and age, law enforcement has to be open to changing that situation.

I believe the tactical community should go out of its way to cooperate with the media. I know this runs counter to the thinking of many police officers, but I have a logical argument supported by experience.

The media outlets have space and time to fill. When it comes to tactical issues, they have great interest and limited knowledge. Most of the time, they are willing to come to us for information. If we provide it, they go away happy and informed. If we brush them off with a terse "No comment," they still have space and time to fill. In the absence of accurate information from reliable sources, they will be only too happy to listen to any so called "expert" who is willing to talk to them. The DC sniper incident was a perfect example of this process. Never have so many had so much to say with so little substance. Each day, dozens of talking heads sat in front of cameras and speculated about things they knew little about.

Care must be taken in agreeing to speak with the media. You must learn the fine art of speaking in sound bites, choosing your words and phrases to carefully convey your message. Long answers to questions tend to fall victim to creative editing. I had a personal experience where the answers I gave to questions on tape, were not matched to the same questions I had answered live.

There is one other caveat to this relationship with the media. In the interest of truth and accuracy, we have an obligation to tell the media, and by extension the public, what we do. However, we have no obligation at all to share with them how we do it. I cringe every time I see some police spokesman giving a tour of the armory on camera, talking about our equipment and how it is applied to certain situations. Again referring to the DC incident, I was approached numerous times by different media outlets with requests to do live fire demonstrations of sniper rifles. Because none of them could give me a good reason why this was necessary, it never happened. But, I'm disappointed to say, others in the field obliged them.

Part of it is ego. Some people develop a sense of importance from standing in the spotlight and sounding knowledgeable. But never forget the reason for limiting the information you broadcast. Your next callout is sitting in that audience. He is learning about your team, its equipment, tactics and capabilities by watching you. Every bit of information you give him, adds to his advantage in your next confrontation.

A better approach is to give the media a few bits of general, knowledge information and leave it at that. They won't know any better, and don't have the background to ask the right questions. Feed them the information you want them to have, and hold them accountable for what they report. Let them know if they don't report the facts, they won't be provided with any information in the future.

A sidebar: In Fall, 2002, the so-called "DC Sniper" incident brought enormous attention to the legitimate sniper community from the media. During that three-week span, I was fielding 20 to 30 phone calls a day, and nearly as many emails, from various media outlets, asking questions ranging from the simple to the silly. I learned a great deal about dealing with the media during that stretch. I gained insight into how they think and work.

Immediately after the capture of the culprits, the phone calls stopped instantly. As the media is prone to do, snipers were no longer interesting and they were off to their next sensational topic. Because much of the media contact was initiated through the ASA website, I felt compelled to post an open letter to the media, first to answer some of the persistent questions reporters were asking. I thought it might be beneficial to include it here for future reference.

OPEN LETTER TO THE MEDIA

Since the arrests of John Mohammad and John Lee Malvo, our phones have gone quiet. The media, with its short attention span, has moved on to other hot topics. Suddenly, the "sniper community" is no longer an issue, important or interesting. Still, we will leave this message posted in advance of the next rifle-toting serial killer. The circumstances of the incident may change, but its relation to the professional sniper community will not.

When you want to talk to real snipers about the reality of their job, we will be happy to spend time with you. In the interim, we would like to list, for the record, our official positions on many of the topics raised.

• A professional sniper is a specially selected, specially trained, specially equipped team member, who makes use of his skills, training and equipment to gain a position of advantage, and provide real time information to his tactical team, to aid them in planning and executing a peaceful resolution to a critical incident. As a secondary function, the sniper provides lethal cover and protection to team members, innocent civilians, and hostages, and if necessary, can direct precision fire against designated authorized targets.

• The mission of the professional sniper is to save and safeguard lives.

• The individuals responsible for the string of killings in the DC area were not snipers, in the true sense of the word. They were serial killers who used a rifle to indiscriminately kill innocent civilians from a concealed position. In this context, these were the actions of cowards, not armed professionals. These were evil men committing evils deeds. Even they haven't offered a better rationale for their actions.

• ASA does not provide sniper training of any kind to private citizens. There is no good reason why a civilian needs to learn sniper skills. Although there are schools, which will provide this type of training for a fee, ASA does not endorse them. There are those who have labeled us "anti-American", as well as less flattering names because of this, but our beliefs are built on reason and experience, and we stand by them.

• We recognize the existence of the so-called sniper subculture. We know about the groupies, wannabes and enthusiasts to whom this is a hobby and a weekend fantasy. For the trained professionals we represent, this is our job. We do not take this lightly or view it as a game.

• The skills the shooters displayed during this incident did not lend credence to theories that they had special training or capabilities. Background investigations since their arrest have confirmed this. Anyone can learn to shoot a rifle with a fair degree of accuracy. Nor is there anything extraordinary about the rifle or the round they were shooting. Both are popular and easily obtained by sportsman, competitive shooters and varmint hunters.

• This is not a crime that could have been prevented or solved by more restrictive laws. You can't keep guns out of the hands of people determined to use them for crimes. You can't legislate morality or conscience. We don't endorse the knee-jerk reactionaries who want to ban sniper rifles, schools and other items. Enforce the laws that exist.

• The law enforcement agencies involved in this case did their best to solve it as soon as possible. This was an extremely difficult situation, unlike anything else in law enforcement. Few agencies are adequately prepared to handle such a large scale and fluid engagement. Hopefully, the lessons learned from this will help to prepare agencies everywhere for the next one.

• Professional snipers have been working in the police tactical community for over thirty years. Our actions on operations have saved thousands of lives. Why has it taken three decades and a series of tragedies for the media to suddenly decide we merit attention?

Not everyone in society has what it takes to become a police officer. Not every police officer has what it takes to become a SWAT team member. And not every SWAT member has what it takes to be a sniper. This is a career pinnacle. These men and women have demonstrated an exceptional commitment to their team, agency and the public they are sworn to protect. They are not trained killers, rogue warriors or "scary people." Snipers are ordinary people, who have taken on an extraordinary job. The title "sniper" is one we wear with pride. Real snipers save lives, every time they go to work. How many of you can make the same claim?

CONTROVERSY

Let's face it, in the vast majority of police sniper operations, if everything goes right, the team will come, do their job, and withdraw, and no one will ever know they were on scene. The only time snipers attract attention is when someone dies and/or someone screws up. In either case, the attention is usually cast in a negative light and teams find themselves having to defend their actions. Why does it happen and what can be done about it? Looking at the issue objectively, I feel the roots of controversial sniper operations are in execution or elocution.

The execution problems are manifested in equipment issues, training and tactics. For example, a callout in Texas a few years ago resulted in the accidental death of an entry officer. His own sniper shot him in the head. One of the contributing factors in the tragedy was the sniper's rifle, which had a trigger pull weight of less than a pound and a half. This is viewed as a clear violation of industry standards for sniper rifles, and therefore hard to defend. A controversial sniper incident possibly has a different outcome with the use of proper equipment.

In another incident, a young hostage is shot and dumped outside his door, and a sniper on the scene does nothing to prevent it. Why? The shooting took place in a darkened doorway. The sniper did not have night vision capabilities and simply could not see what was happening. Just having the right equipment may have altered the outcome.

Training, or the lack thereof, has led to SWAT teams employing questionable tactics. Each time a team is faced with circumstances they haven't trained for, they are forced to improvise. Maybe they take no action at all, because they aren't sure what to do. Examples have been seen in callouts involving intermediate barriers, low-light shootings, and sniper initiated assaults, just to name a few. If your team hasn't practiced these, chances are very good something very bad can happen. It is important you become a student of history and make your team aware of the types of situations teams around the country are facing. Using those situations as templates, you must train for every imaginable contingency, so as to be prepared ahead of time. Trial and error has no place in a tactical operation.

Sometimes, it's not what we do, but what we say that sparks the controversy. Referring again to the incident in Texas, the sniper in question raised eyebrows when his official report completely contradicted eyewitness accounts and the physical evidence at the scene. A sniper in Wisconsin responded to a call involving a suicidal subject sitting in a vehicle with a gun. After frantic attempts to negotiate a peaceful resolution with the subject, he decided to escalate the situation. He exited the vehicle with a loaded shotgun and, ignoring directions to the contrary, pointed the gun in the direction of a SWAT officer. The sniper, feeling his teammate was in imminent danger, shot and killed the man. The evening news led with a video clip and a report questioning the justification for the shot. It seems they interviewed some police official who wasn't at the scene, but was quoted saying there were no officers in the area placed in danger when the subject lowered his shotgun. Therefore, the shot was being viewed as unnecessary. As a result, the next day, the Chief himself is on camera doing damage control, explaining to the uninformed how SWAT personnel were deployed and pointing out a specific officer in the line of fire who was saved by the sniper's action.

While controversy in tactical operations can't always be avoided, it can be squelched quickly with decisive action on the part of the agency. In Texas, a nice young man was shot and killed by a police sniper. He was only shooting a .22 rifle randomly in his neighborhood, then in the direction of the first police officers on the scene. So when he was killed, the media was only too happy to focus on questions from friends and family as to why he couldn't have been simply wounded in an arm or leg. To his credit, the Chief of Police held a news conference and stated for all to hear his sniper is not trained to shoot to wound. He said his officers are trained to use deadly force to quickly stop a threat. End of controversy.

Opening a newscast with, "SWAT responded to a situation today and everything went fine," is not going to glue viewers to their seats, and media moguls know that. It serves their interests to always look for a hook for a story. Questioning the justification of police actions is a sure way to garner attention. We know they will never let the truth get in the way of a good story. The most effective counter action for your agency is to get the facts out as soon as possible. Information from a reliable source quickly dispels the rumors and innuendoes.

Controversial sniper operations are going to happen. But we can minimize their frequency and their impact with preparation and education. Well-trained snipers using good equipment and employing proper tactics will perform professionally. Their actions in operations will leave little room for criticism. Make the effort to address the public and educate them about how SWAT operations really work. Their perceptions of your profession come from television shows and movies. Be willing to confront the media and don't allow them to get away with twisting the facts or reporting half-truths.

It all sounds so simple. Why is it so hard to do?

WAR STORIES

"What has once happened will invariably happen again, when
the circumstances which combined to produce it, shall again
combine in the same way." —Abraham Lincoln

Those who refuse to learn from history are doomed to repeat it. We
have all heard this quotation, yet still many in the tactical community
ignore its message. As I teach in various venues around the country, I
present videotapes and case studies of incidents involving snipers.
Afterwards, I usually ask the audience if they are familiar with the incident. Most of the time, the majority have not seen or heard anything
about it.

This raises two concerns for me. First, I have always felt snipers,
and the people in charge of them, need to be students of their art.
This includes doing study and research on your own. The incidents I
present are available from a variety of news sources. I found them by
looking for them. Every serious sniper should be doing the same thing.
You have to be aware of what is happening in the tactical community.
Training has to extend beyond that one day on the range.

Secondly, information is worthless if it isn't shared. What happens
to any one team in the community proves it can happen to any other
team. Therefore, every team should be studying these incidents, and
learning the lessons they offer. But this is not happening. The evidence is the number of teams still repeating the mistakes of others.

Police agencies are notorious in their "it worked so it must be okay"
attitude. You've all seen it. A team or an officer does something really
stupid, reckless, and/or dangerous. Somehow, they get through it and
things turn out okay. A smart person would say, "That was dumb. I'll
never do that again." Cops pat themselves on the back and tell each
other what a great job they did. I've even seen instances where officers

have received commendations for stupid actions. A friend of mine once wrote, "Good results reinforce poor practices." Police officers are far from perfect, and we do ourselves a disservice when we refuse to own our mistakes and learn from them. The only way we will get better at our job is to take an unflinching look at what we do and how we do it. The facts are the facts and speak for themselves. We need to look at our experiences objectively and draw the good and bad from them. War stories hold a wealth of information, if we are willing to look and listen.

This chapter retells some of those stories. Details of each case are drawn from firsthand knowledge, personal interviews, and after-action reports. In many cases, the snipers themselves proffer the lessons learned. It is not my intention to second-guess any of the agencies represented here. My objective is to present the incidents as they happened, give you the facts impartially, and point out the lessons learned in each case. Hopefully, you will take the time to study them and learn from the experiences of others.

To help maintain objectivity, no persons or agencies are identified in these case studies. However, I want to thank those who cared enough about the community to willingly share their stories, warts and all.

Case Study #1 – A car chase in the Southeast started this callout. Several subjects were interrupted during a residential burglary, jumped into a get away car, and took off with officers in pursuit. The car crashed a short time later, and the occupants bailed out. One subject is taken into custody right away, but the other two disappeared into the neighborhood.

A short time later, a 911 call from a witness led to the arrest of subject #2 hiding nearby. A K-9 officer spotted the third bad guy run into another house. A perimeter is quickly set up. The police on scene find out the bad guy is armed and holding three people inside hostage. SWAT is called.

One of the snipers shows up with the first members of the team. Knowing his job, he deploys in a building about 50 yards away, and begins passing on information. His partner arrives at the command post a short time later. However, as he is getting dressed out, the team commander tells him he doesn't need a sniper at that moment. Instead, the commander tells the sniper to get ready to go with the entry team.

The first sniper is made aware of this development by radio. The sniper responded with a few terse words and finally the commander relented, letting the second sniper gear up and go to his partner. However, when he unpacked his rifle, he found a round loaded backwards in his detachable magazine, and the magazine in his rifle. Understandably, this was a disconcerting moment, instantly planting doubts in the mind of the sniper, because he knows someone has been handling his weapon.

The callout is later resolved when the bad guy surrenders, but there were issued raised that resulted in a rather heated debriefing session afterwards. First, the team commander obviously had no understanding of the role a sniper team is expected to play in the overall SWAT team matrix. The primary role of the sniper is to provide eyes on, real time information. No tactical operation can be run at optimum efficiency and safety without this. Still, he had attempted to take a sniper away from his duties to fill a spot on an entry team. This is not an uncommon situation. Far too many teams are undermanned; trying to make do with eight, ten, twelve officers, when history has shown a higher number is needed. I understand manpower constraints, especially in smaller agencies. There is no simple answer to this dilemma. However, teams and agencies need to look at the pros and cons of a small team.

The second issue is the security of the sniper's weapon. I have always been an advocate of giving each sniper sole possession of his rifle. He should be allowed to keep it in his possession, or be able to lock it up in a secure area to which only he has access. Those are the only ways the sniper can be sure no one has tampered with his weapon since he shot it last.

The backward round in the magazine was worrisome, but unlikely to cause a weapon malfunction. This was a condition the sniper would (should) instantly notice as he made his weapon ready for service. But realizing someone has touched his gun would completely undermine a sniper's confidence. Who has touched the gun and what else did he screw up? Whether someone with malicious intent tampered with the gun, or just a moron matters little. The impact is still the same. The sniper will not be able to trust his gun until he can go to the range and verify its performance. Some would call us anal. I like to think of it as being thorough. Bottom line is no one other than the sniper needs to have access to his gun, without his permission or knowledge, ever.

Case Study # 2 – Deputies responding to a call of a man chasing his wife with a rifle came under fire when they arrived on the scene. The man barricaded himself behind his house, behind a pickup truck. SWAT was called right away. A perimeter was set up and a negotiator made contact with the subject via PA.

Snipers were deployed in two separate positions, one at 50 yards, the other at approximately 60 yards, triangulating on the subject's truck. Their close proximity to the subject allowed them to overhear much of the negotiation dialogue. Among other things, he boasted about his shooting ability.

The subject had a supply of beers, as well as his rifle, lying on the seat of the pickup truck. The snipers watched him as he would reach into the truck numerous times to pick up a beer, drink from it, and put it back down on the seat. On several occasions, he picked up the rifle instead of a beer, but was careful not to shoulder it, or present it in any threatening manners. Each time, he put the rifle back on the seat and resumed negotiations.

After about 45 minutes, the subject started to show signs of increasing agitation. Without warning, he picked up the rifle, and in one fluid motion, raised it and fired a shot at the negotiators. The snipers reacted immediately to the subject's action. One sniper fired a shot, which struck the subject in the chest and killed him.

The snipers themselves brought up three issues they felt were important lessons learned and worth discussing. First, was the question, "should a subject who has already fired at a police officer be allowed to hold a weapon under any circumstances?" In this case, he had already displayed a willingness to shoot at the police, was becoming increasingly intoxicated, and showing no signs of surrendering. Each time he touched his weapon, the snipers found themselves in a reactionary mode. They felt it gave an advantage to the shooter.

Second, they allowed the subject's actions to eventually lower their threat perception and lull them into a routine. Over and over, the subject would reach into the cab of his truck, and most of the time he would retrieve a beer. A few times he picked up the rifle, but never held it up in any aggressive manner. Seeing these non-threatening actions over and over lulled them into a false sense of safety.

Last, the value of triangulating on a subject paid off. When the subject raised his rifle to shoot, he leaned forward. In doing so, his body position shifted to a point where the view of one of the two snipers was blocked by a tree. At the moment of truth, he had no shot. The fortunate positioning of the second sniper gave them the ability to protect the negotiators with a quick reactionary shot.

Case Study # 3 – A high-risk warrant service leads us to the next hard-learned lesson. The plan as laid out in the briefing called for the sniper to set up an observation point giving him a view of the front door in advance of the entry team. Once in place, his responsibilities included observation of the target location and protection of the team as they made their approach. The team was going to make a stealth approach, using a rental truck to deliver the team to the front door of the residence. Prior to leaving their jump off point, the entry team was supposed to notify the sniper by radio.

The sniper set up in a field across the street from his target. However, because of vegetation and elevation, he found he could not clearly see the front door of the house. He did have a clear line of sight to the second floor.

While he was still in the process of settling into his position, the sniper was alerted to the approach of an unmarked delivery truck. It didn't match the description of the truck he was expecting to see, but he noticed the back door was raised a few inches, and he could see what looked like booted feet of several individuals inside. A quick radio inquiry informed him the entry team had just arrived.

The sniper now needed to scramble because his current position did not meet his operational responsibilities. The team was disembarking and he still could not cover the front door or anything on the ground level. He grabbed his rifle and attempted to resituate it. Something, possibly some of the heavy vegetation, snagged on the weapon, preventing him from swinging the gun laterally. He twisted a little harder to clear the snag and heard the rifle discharge. On the ground below, the entry team immediately reacted to the sound of shots fired. The sniper had to go on the air to tell them the shot was his, and they could proceed with their approach and entry. The team finished their assault without incident. The sniper, on the other hand, had to work out what just happened.

Fortunately, no one was injured, but he was still confused and more than a little embarrassed. The subsequent investigation found the round struck the front of the house and lodged there. What is believed to have happened is when the sniper tried to move his rifle, it became entangled in the vegetation. When he applied more force to clear the obstruction, something came in contact with the trigger and caused the weapon to discharge. The sniper insisted his finger was never inside the trigger guard.

There are several issues raised here. Should the bolt have been closed on a live round with the entry team now in the sniper's line of fire? What is their policy and practice on this? What is yours? Some teams feel as soon as friendly personnel are in the line of fire, the snipers make their weapons safe and come off target.

What does your team consider safe? Some snipers rely on the mechanical safety on the weapon. Others practice making the weapon safe by lifting the bolt handle. The better method is the one you train with and use religiously.

An independent investigation revealed the trigger weight on the rifle in question was about 1.5 pounds. This is pretty much recognized as far too light for tactical work. The rifle was a Remington 700, owned by the department. Amazingly, no one in the agency knew for sure who did the gunsmithing work on the trigger, or when.

The ASA printed a well-researched Position Paper addressing trigger pull weights. Officially, a trigger weight of 3.5 to 4.5 pounds is deemed to practical, reasonable, and legally defensible. Triggers lighter than 3.5 pounds can be problematic, especially in the hands of snipers with limited experience. The danger of accidental and negligent discharges increases as the trigger weight decreases. The perceived advantage of a lighter trigger is negated by the potential hazard to a sniper. Adding operational factors like stress, cold hands, gloves, or obstructions can increase the danger.

The last issue was the lack of documentation of the work done to the weapon. Apparently both of the department's sniper rifles had been modified, but no records could be found identifying the gunsmith or when the work was done. Letting an unqualified gunsmith do anything more than admire your weapon is a mistake. These are specialized tools and require attention from someone with knowledge and skills. Keep the local gun plumber away from your weapon. And everything done to your gun has to be carefully documented. This includes cleanings, maintenance and repairs. Your data book is a good place for this documentation to be recorded. Then, as department guns are passed on to the new snipers as they come on the team, the data book should follow the gun. Thus each subsequent owner will know the gun's history. The idea of sniper weapons being online with no reliable records of modifications is unacceptable in our world.

Could the negligent discharge have been prevented? Yes. Hopefully, the discharge and all of the circumstances leading to it will be learning points for other snipers.

Case Study #4 - On some occasions, timing is everything. A west coast gang member on a mission showed up at an area high school. He was not a student and was told to leave the campus by school personnel and the school resource officer. About thirty minutes later, he returned. As a female student exited a car in the parking lot, the subject yells out a gang slogan, produces a handgun and fires three rounds into the car. The car speeds off and the subject grabs the female in a headlock. He drags her at gunpoint into the school quad area.

The lunchtime crowd mingling in the quad sees what is going on and flees in panic. The school resource officer confronts the subject and tries to negotiate with him. The subject continues to clutch the young girl by the neck, alternately pressing the gun against her head and waving it at other persons in the immediate area. The resource officer realizes the danger of the situation, but feels he has no shot because of his distance from the subject, and the close proximity of the hostage. He puts out a radio call for help and does what he can to stabilize his situation until it arrives.

SWAT just happens to have been out training that afternoon. When the first calls went out, they were returning to a training site and quickly rerouted to the school. Other patrol officers were responding and setting up containment around the campus. In the meantime, the standoff in the quad area continued.

The first two SWAT officers arrive in the same car a few minutes later. They grab their equipment from the trunk of the car and head for the quad. One of the two is a sniper. He runs with his long gun in its case, followed by a partner sporting an MP-5. They come to a spot adjacent to the quad area. The sniper retrieves his rifle, prones out and sets up. Looking through his scope, he immediately recognizes the subject as an imminent threat, as he is pressing a cocked handgun to the head of his hostage. He waits long enough to assure a safe shot on an erratic target. A single headshot from 55 yards instantly ends the subject's threat. The shot is taken 53 seconds from the time the sniper arrived on scene.

I can't say enough good things about this incident. The sniper did an outstanding job under stressful conditions. He had a motivated and dangerous hostage taker, holding a hostage in close proximity. The sniper focused on the task at hand and followed the rules of the target engagement sequence we teach in class. In quick succession, he acquired and identified his target. He took the time to isolate that target in space, making sure he had a clear line of flight to his target and a safe background. Only then did he engage his target with one well-placed round. His decisive actions undoubtedly saved lives that day.

This incident has also provided validation for an important teaching point. For years, we have incorporated stress drills into our schools and competitions. Having snipers sprint various distances and engage targets while their hearts are still racing has been a training staple. However, from the very beginning, I have always heard some sniper grumble about the reality of that type of shooting. "I would never run and shoot that fast," is a fair paraphrase of the complaint/excuse. Finally, I have a definitive comeback.

Fifty-three seconds.

Case Study #5 – As with so many SWAT calls, the ending of a bad relationship was the triggering event for this incident in the northwest. An estranged husband walked into a bar where his wife was sitting, drinking with a number friends. When he produced a gun and began firing shots, panic ensued. Several patrons were able to run out the door to safety. Others, including the wife were held hostage at gunpoint. Responding police units quickly assessed the situation and SWAT was soon on scene.

During the course of negotiations, the subject released his remaining hostages, including his wife. The standoff has evolved into an armed barricade.

The front door of the bar has been left standing open. The team pulled their armored vehicle up to a position about 25 yards away from the bar. Because it is the only place that affords him a line of sight into the bar, the sniper decides to use the APC as his shooting platform. He has to assume a position, standing up in the open hatch of the vehicle, with his custom rifle setting on the roof.

The decision was made to make entry. In preparation, the assault team stacked near the open door. It was then the subject appeared behind the bar. The sniper saw him aim his handgun in the direction where he anticipated the team would enter. Fearing for their safety, and knowing only he had a vantage point to intervene from, the sniper sighted in on the subject and pulled the trigger on his rifle. Instead of the expected bang, flash and recoil, the sniper heard only a metallic click. Training took over and kept him from lingering too long while the shock registered. He cycled his bolt, came back on target, and this time fired a round into the face of the subject before he could shoot at the point man he'd spotted. He fell lifeless behind the bar.

Years of good habits, reinforced with repetition in training, paid huge dividends here. His malfunction in the midst of a critical moment was dealt with quickly and decisively, resulting in a positive outcome. The question on everyone's mind though is what happened?

There are several theories being circulated. However, the one given the most credence was demonstrated for us by master riflesmith Charlie Milazzo. It is possible with Remington actions to close the bolt on a live round and have the bolt handle raised just enough above its locked down position to cause a misfire. Pulling the trigger will cause the bolt handle to snap down to the locked position, the striker will fall, and you may even get a light strike on the primer. However, the strike will not be sufficient enough to detonate the round.

Operationally, make sure the bolt handle is completely down. Check it occasionally, as it is possible to accidentally nudge it out of position and not know it. Always plan for quick and smooth transitions and follow up shots. Practice shooting from awkward and unusual positions as well. This should include using vehicles as a shooting platform. As seen here, the APC provided the best vantage point for observation and cover. Standing in an open hatch is not one of your classic range positions. Get off the bipods and train for the real world.

Case Study #6 – A running gun battle during a high-speed chase set the stage for a unique sniper engagement in the Northwest. The suspect fired shots at pursuing units from his sunroof as he sped along the interstate. The multi-jurisdictional chase came to an end when an officer was able to spike the vehicle's tires.

The subject was seen fleeing from the vehicle and into a nearby wood line. Witnesses reported he was armed, although there was some confusion about the type of weapon. Initial reports had him carrying a rifle. Officers converged on the car and quickly surrounded the area. SWAT and patrol elements set up a hasty perimeter, complete with sniper coverage, and began a controlled search for the shooter.

Without warning, the subject emerged from the woods near one of the perimeter positions. The officers challenged him, but he refused to step out into the open or surrender. Instead, he remained partially concealed in the heavy underbrush. The snipers on scene moved into positions that allowed them a better line of sight. One took up a spot about 30 yards from the subject. Another set up approximately 70 yards away. A third was running to a better spot when the shots rang out.

The subject had been actively ignoring verbal commands and calls to surrender. Suddenly, he reached behind his back and raised what looked like a handgun. Two snipers recognized the threat simultaneously and fired in response. Their shots sounded like one. The subject was struck by both rounds and died instantly.

Two things made this shooting unique. The spontaneous, simultaneous engagement was one of the first of its kind. Second, the sniper positioned 70 yards from the subject was faced with a dilemma. He tried to establish a stable strong side, prone position. However, he could not find a way to lay prone, shouldering his rifle strong side, which would provide him adequate cover. Concerned for his safety, as he should be with an armed subject, he chose to take up a weak side position. When the time came, the sniper was forced to take his shot using his weak side shoulder. His shot went between several trees and branches, and struck the subject in the ear. It was the first time he had ever shot using his weak shoulder.

Their incident clearly illustrated the need to diversify your range training. Snap shooting under tight time constraints, coordinated shots, and shooting from unorthodox positions, including weak shoulder, all need to be practiced. You will not hesitate to employ a technique on a callout if you have developed confidence in your ability to execute it through training. Train for the real world.

Case Study # 7 – As distasteful as it is to second guess the actions of another sniper, if we are afraid to point out a mistake, then mistakes will continue to be repeated. Small mistakes can be embarrassing ego bruisers, larger mistakes can be fatal. Hopefully, by calling attention to this incident, the mistakes made here won't ever be repeated.

A SWAT team was doing a day of scenario training at a local bus depot. The morning session was dedicated mostly to entry teamwork. Lunchtime came, and the team leader asked the sniper to go to the station to retrieve his rifle. The plan was to incorporate the sniper into the afternoon scenarios. The sniper did as he was asked, collecting his rifle from the SWAT locker and returning to his spot outside the depot. He set the rifle up on its bipod and decided to spend the time waiting for training to resume doing some dry fire. According to his report, he took the magazine out of the weapon, and sighted in on a team leader sitting in the front seat of a bus in the depot. The sniper pulled the trigger and the weapon discharged. The round struck the team leader in the head, killing him instantly.

The sniper and his teammates were stunned. The effect on the department and their community was devastating. However, the nightmare was just beginning. A follow up investigation into the incident led to suspension and criminal charges being filed against the sniper. In addition to everything else that had occurred, he was now facing losing his job and the possibility of going to prison.

What happened? Obviously, there was a round left in the chamber of the rifle when the sniper pulled the trigger. There have been different versions of the chain of events that led to the round getting there, and I believe the only person who really knows the truth is the sniper. So, I won't waste time speculating on that. What is undeniable is the fact there was a round in the chamber, the sniper pointed his rifle at his team leader, and then pulled the trigger without first determining with certainty the condition of his weapon. This is unacceptable.

Given the sequence of events leading up to the shooting, there were so many points when the weapon should have been checked. The rifle should never have been stored with a live round under a closed bolt. To me, this means the sniper was negligent in putting the gun away. More troubling is bringing the gun into a training environment, and not ascertaining the gun was clear, safe and empty before interacting with other team members. The fault here belongs to the sniper, as well as the safety officer overseeing the exercise.

Dry fire is recognized as a legitimate training tool. Tracking a living target is a necessary skill, and there is no other way to accurately duplicate it. Plus, it is critical a sniper become acclimated to seeing real people in his scope. However, pointing a scoped rifle at a human being in a training scenario needs to be done only under close supervision. The weapon has to be cleared, verified by multiple persons, and rendered safe before being employed in this manner. Anything less stringent invites disaster. How does someone decide to use a rifle to dry fire without cycling the bolt at least once? How do you determine the weapon is clear safe and empty without looking into the chamber? Whether it was laziness, carelessness or incompetence, the result was the death of one police officer at the hands of a friend, and a life-changing event for all who survived him.

The sniper eventually agreed to a plea bargain, which kept him out of jail, but his career as a police officer is over forever. Family, friends and fellow officers have been traumatized. Outsiders have scrutinized SWAT training procedures and criticized some practices. The ripples from this event continue to flow.

Someone once told me SWAT cops are the worst offenders when it comes to range safety. He felt their cockiness made them careless; after all, they handle guns all the time. He suggested reminding them they were even more likely to have an accident, *because* they handle guns all the time.

Safety is the responsibility of everyone. During the year this incident occurred, eight SWAT officers were injured or killed by friendly fire. This is a danger area we have complete control over. All it takes is attention to details. Have policies and procedures in place for weapon handling during training exercises, and follow them to the letter. In all situations, know the condition of your weapon. No one ever got hurt by being too cautious. Accidents damage the team's confidence in one another, as well as the public's confidence in them. Added to the possible loss of life, the cost of carelessness is far too high.

Case Study #8 – A hostage standoff in a Northeastern highway rest stop started a week earlier and a thousand miles away. The male suspect had brazenly walked into a beauty shop and kidnapped his estranged girlfriend at gunpoint. They were last seen leaving the area in a car. What followed was a cross-country bus ride, with him holding the girlfriend in submission with threats of death to herself and her family if she tried to escape. She rode with him in terrorized silence for days, until a lapse in his attention allowed her an opportunity to slip a note to the bus driver. Made aware of the situation behind him, the driver engineered a ruse that led him to stopping his bus in the rest area and contacting the police.

Waiting anxiously in the parking lot, the suspect reacted to the arrival of police officers by producing a gun and pressing it against the head of his hostage. The officers backed off, called for help and the drama began in earnest.

SWAT personnel converged on the scene, including a number of snipers. They set up containment while negotiators tried vainly to talk the suspect into a peaceful resolution. He chose to maintain a headlock on his girlfriend and continued threats against her life.

One sniper stalked into a position in the wood line behind the rest stop area. He slid into a hide that gave him a clear line of sight to where the suspect and the hostage were standing in the open parking lot. The estranged couple stood in their hostile embrace while he checked with his laser rangefinder and determined the distance to be 187 yards. They presented a profile target to him. The hostage was closest to him. The boyfriend was behind her. Her head was pressed against his left cheek as he held his left arm round her throat. In his right hand, he held a cocked semiautomatic pistol, which was now pointed at her head. His hooded sweatshirt was pulled up, obscuring most of his face. The sniper dialed in the appropriate dope corrections in his scope and settled in for the wait.

The suspect was not cooperating with the negotiators, and they were not hopeful. They limited his action options. He could not get back on the bus with the gun and the hostage. To allow that would put her and any tactical officers attempting a hostage rescue at great risk. He was repeatedly offered the choice of peaceful surrender, but he steadfastly refused to take it.

Finally, he elected to take action. He tightened his chokehold and lifted his hostage up on her toes. He shuffled forward a few steps in the direction of the bus then stopped. The sniper knew the couple was not to be allowed to return to the bus and watched as they approached the point of no return. As he locked onto his target, his crosshairs settled on the impression of the suspect's left ear under the hood. When the suspect started shuffling forward again, the sniper pressed the trigger and sent his shot downrange. The round covered the distance in a heartbeat and ended the suspect's life before his back hit the pavement. His liberated girlfriend pulled free of his limp grip and ran to safety.

The shot itself was extraordinary. At 187 yards, it is one of the longest single sniper shots recorded in modern police operations. The round literally went over the top of the hostage's head to reach its intended target. A miscalculation by the sniper could have resulted in the accidental death of his hostage. Their shuffling movement simply increased the degree of difficulty.

In his debriefing, the sniper displayed an attitude some would describe as cocky. He said he never had any doubts about making his shot, and called its placement exactly. I believe a good sniper has to be a little cocky. To me, cockiness is confidence built on a foundation of demonstrated skill. He knew his rifle, his scope, and had trained at distances similar to this situation. He had made this shot hundreds of times in practice. In his mind, there was no reason to doubt his ability to make the shot. His mental approach was exactly what a successful sniper needs.

This incident is a graphic illustration of the importance of realistic, job-specific sniper training. Training must reflect the skills a tactical sniper will need in the field. This includes various distances, partially obscured targets, and moving targets. Careful study of the types of engagements snipers are facing in operations will serve as an outline for your training program. Once again, the importance of sharing information with the sniper community should be clear.

Case Study #9 – Where the previous case looked at the longest sniper engagement, this one ranks as one of the shortest.

As happens too many times, this incident began with a domestic clash. A son with a long criminal past and a drug habit attacked his mother during an argument. He grabbed a knife and threatened to slice her up. Another child in the apartment was awakened by the confrontation and called the police. The first officers responded and were met by the unwelcome sight of the deranged man holding his mother in a headlock, with a large knife poised near her throat. They wisely held their ground and called for SWAT.

A negotiator and an assault unit took up a position inside the apartment, replacing the patrol officers. The son held his mother in a cramped interior hallway, just outside the bathroom. As the negotiator tried to reason with the son, he taunted the police and tortured his mother, prodding her with the knife. Because of where the standoff was occurring inside the apartment, traditional sniper deployment was useless. Instead, two snipers came into the apartment and set up in the hall, behind the assault team officers, and offered what support they could. Unfortunately, from their vantage point, they could see little, could shoot at even less.

Ahead of them in the hall, the two assault team officers participated in a bizarre death dance with the suspect. They were trying in vain to maneuver into a position to get a shot at him. He was fully aware of their intentions, and frustrated them by clutching his frantic mother close, and peaking out from behind her head to verbally challenge them. He was completely ignoring the negotiators pleas for surrender. He raised the level of violence by probing his mother with the knife, deep enough to draw screams and blood.

Sensing the escalating danger and knowing the inability of his teammates to find a clear and safe shot, one of the snipers made a bold decision. He left his position and moved in close behind the entry officers. He whispered to one of them to hold still and rested his rifle on the teammate's shoulder. In the next few seconds, the dance came to a sudden end. The son made the mistake of peeking a little too far, for too long. The sniper took advantage of the opportunity and fired a single round into the son's head, ending his night of terror. Justice was delivered from a distance of five yards.

The sniper said the shot, while challenging, was attempted with confidence (there's that word again) because his team has often practiced shooting up close, and shooting from a variety of platforms, including people. Prior training had taught him to turn down his scope power and how to best work with a partner to attain a stable standing position. In a stressful life and death encounter, he simply reverted to his training and accomplished his mission.

Another issue in this incident was lighting, or lack of. The standoff occurred in a darkened hallway. At the beginning, the only light available was a small overhead light in the bathroom, which cast the son and mother in a dim silhouette. A tactical consideration the team is looking at for future operations is a way of attaching a light to their sniper weapons in a quick detachable fashion. This would be a special application for a unique set of circumstances. However, this incident should make everyone aware of another contingency for which to plan and train.

Case Study # 10 – This last incident serves as a cold reminder of the thankless nature of our chosen profession.

SWAT team members responded to an armed barricade. A suicidal female was sitting in her car, brandishing a cocked handgun. This particular individual was a frequent flyer, as the team had been called to similar standoffs with her on three prior occasions. Usually, she got drunk, made threats until she sobered up, then surrendered peacefully. This night would be different.

The sniper showed up an hour after his team had deployed. He was the victim of a pager system that failed to work properly (that never happens). He and his partner stalked across an open field to set up in a prone position about 70 yards from the passenger side door of the car.

The decision had been made to push this standoff to a quick resolution. A team contingent closed on the rear of the car and fired a gas canister at the rear window. Unfortunately, because of the angle, the projectile bounced off and landed in the field. The impact shattered the window and obscured their view into the vehicle. This was important because when they approached closer to fire a second round, they could not see the driver swing around in her seat and bring the gun up to bear on them. The sniper did. He fired a single, well-aimed shot into the back of her head. In killing her, the sniper saved the lives of his teammates.

The sniper went through the usual post shooting rituals. He survived the interviews that night with little difficulty. Thanks to a supportive family, team and friends, he got through the next few days as well. He faced some unique challenges during his Grand Jury experience, but was ultimately cleared and his shooting was ruled justified. All investigations were closed and the case was disposed of.

The sniper thought his experience would be beneficial to others and was conscientious enough to decide to write a book about it. He talked it over with his chief and received his blessing. The sniper wrote a book that went into great detail about his perspective and thoughts on the incident, but he also went to great lengths to be discreet. He never identifies his agency, or any of the principals. This anonymity allowed him to be brutally honest about all aspects of his experience without bringing undue embarrassment to any of the involved parties. The facts are the facts, and the story speaks for itself. The book is enlightening for most, and a mirror for others.

I won't steal any of the author's thunder by going into the details explored in the book. I recommend you read it for yourself. It is listed in the Recommended Reading section.

Like so many other police officers at the time, the sniper was called to active duty and went away to serve his country for a year. While he was away, the book was published. As expected, it got great reviews and sold very well. Readers were afforded the vicarious exposure to the sniper's ultimate experience. By preparing others for what they might face, the sniper may be saving more lives.

The sniper comes home from his deployment and returns to work. However, instead of a warm welcome, he is greeted with the news that he is on administrative leave, pending a criminal investigation into possible contempt of court charges. He is told, by writing his book, he may have violated the law by revealing secret Grand Jury information. Now remember, this is years after the case has been properly disposed of and all of the pertinent investigations have been closed. This was also done with full knowledge and permission of his Chief, who was allowed to read early drafts of the material.

It seems some thin-skinned individuals couldn't handle a critical assessment of their actions, and decided to strike back in this ludicrous manner. An officer who had saved lives with his heroic actions was now facing fines, discipline, and the loss of his job. In his absence, he had been the victim of a cowardly betrayal by his own administration.

After several weeks of investigation and negotiations, the final outcome was the sniper paid a fine and was forced to resign from his job.

The choice to resign was at the discretion of the sniper, who felt he was a marked man in his agency. He would seek employment elsewhere.

Given the benefit of 20/20 hindsight, would the sniper have changed anything? You control what you can. He controlled the actions of a dangerous woman and saved the lives of his teammates in the process. He controlled the dissemination of information about his incident, giving an advantage to other snipers who will learn from his experience. He had no control over the actions of others, the people he worked for and with. In his words, he wouldn't have changed a thing. He did the right things for the right reasons. The future will work itself out for the best.

For you, the lesson is a harsh one. Do you really want to be a sniper?

AN EPIPHANY

Life reveals lessons in odd ways and at strange times. Sometimes they come in unexpected moments of clarity.

I had one such moment getting dressed for work one night. As I have every night for as long as I have been a police officer, I was slipping on my ballistic vest. Suddenly, I stopped and looked at my reflection in the mirror. I thought to myself, "who else does this?" Here I was preparing to go to work, and part of my preparation involves putting on body armor. Lying on the bed was my gun belt. In a moment of epiphany, something I had taken for granted for so long suddenly became very clear.

The job of a police officer involves real risk. It is one of the few professions where people are willing to kill you just for showing up. Being a tactical officer raises the level of risk even higher. Among your tools, you carry a gun to work to defend yourself and others.

The lesson I want to pass on to you is simple. Never forget the arena in which we work. From the moment you walk out your door, you are at risk. This is not a game, nor is it a place for poseurs. This is the real world where the stakes are literally measured in life and death. Remember—real bad guys, real bullets, and real blood.

Stay safe. Be ready.

"A close second is not a desirable place to be in a battle to the death." —Chiun, Master of Sinanju

TRADITION

A number of years ago, a sniper friend of mine gave me gift, which I have always treasured. It was special, because of what it represented, and what it meant, both to him and to me. It has become part of a tradition I would like to see spread throughout the sniper community.

We were at dinner one evening during a sniper conference. He announced that he wanted to make a special presentation to some people who were important to him. He gave me a .308 caliber bullet, which had a dented primer, and engraved with my name. When he presented it to me, he said, (and I am paraphrasing here) "This is a gift of protection to someone I consider a special person. Every cop, every soldier, has heard about the 'bullet out there with your name on it.' Now, you are safe, because you have it."

I was sincerely moved by the gesture. To this day, I carry that bullet with me every day. Its tarnished case shows the wear and tear, but its symbolism is in no way diminished. I thought the sentiment was so special, I have since given engraved bullets to my wife, and a small circle of my closest friends.

I encourage each of you to continue the tradition. Give someone you care about a unique token of your respect and affection. And be sure you tell them the story.

A REUNION STORY

A sniper acquaintance once told me this story, and I thought it was appropriate to pass on. It contains a pearl of wisdom.

He had joined the Marine Corps after graduating high school, and had gone to serve in Southeast Asia as a sniper. In fact, he was one of the first Marine snipers to see combat. His tour of duty resulted in numerous engagements, and an attendant body count. He was decorated several times over for his service.

A few years after returning to the world, he was invited to his first high school reunion. He showed up and spent the evening renewing old ties. At one point, he found himself in a conversation with friends and acquaintances, catching up on lost years. Predictably, people were telling one another where they'd been and what they had accomplished in the interim. This one was a lawyer, that one was in business, the usual stories of growing up and maturing. When his turn came around, the sniper told his friends, "I was a Marine sniper in Viet Nam." As was the norm among the Flower Power crowd of the day, one of them recoiled at the admission and said to him, "That's horrible. How could you possibly do that? I mean, what did you feel when you shot and killed those people?"

The sniper said he just shook his head and walked away. He said he couldn't have made them understand what it was like to ride the recoil of a .300 Winchester.

The wise among you will understand the point of his story.

The rest of you will have to ask the wise to explain it to you.

FIGHT THE POWER

"To sin by silence, when we should protest, makes cowards
of men." —Ella Wheeler Wilcox

During a recent class, one student showed up for a fieldcraft exercise wearing woodland camouflage BDUs, which in and of itself is not unusual. He pointed out the fact he would not be wearing this on a real callout, because his team leader insists on all team members wearing black. When I asked why that was the case, he simply said, "Because that is the way it is."

His situation is not unique. Over the years, I have heard lots of snipers tell tales of being required to do certain things simply because a boss has decreed it. Restrictions on rules of engagement, choices in uniforms, limitations on training quantity and content, purchases of equipment are among the most often listed items. Many times the policy is without any realistic rationale. Usually, the reason is some variation of "That's just the way it is." The complaints are far too common in the sniper community, and far too accepted.

I'm telling you what I told him. Nothing will change without effort on our part. If we expect to change the system and the things that are wrong with it, we have to be willing to fight the power. This starts with educating the people in charge. Many of the dumb decisions they make are born out of ignorance. Giving them information about your job and what it takes to do it can make a difference, sometimes. Some bosses refuse to admit to their ignorance; after all, they are in charge. Be persistent. Introducing them to information available in sniper publications and through professional associations will help support your arguments.

In other cases, you simply have to be willing to stand up to them, refusing to continue to do things the wrong way. This can be risky, but in the long run, it is worth it. Document your efforts, putting all requests and recommendations in writing. Send copies to our boss and his boss, and keep copies for your self. Include supporting articles, letters and references. Don't be afraid to call on outside sources as well. Fighting the good fight, with any hope of winning, requires coming with the right ammunition.

A sniper friend once told me he found the motivation to fight the power looking at his infant daughter. He knew how his job and the responsibility placed on him because of it, could ultimately affect her future. Because his program was not receiving the support he felt it needed in order to be safe and successful, he told his new chief he was quitting the team. Instead of wishing him well and showing him the door, his chief was concerned enough to ask why. The sniper took that opportunity to spell out to his boss a litany of complaints, ranging from lack of training and proper equipment, to shaky and questionable leadership. The chief told the sniper things would change under his leadership, and those issues would all be addressed immediately. He was true to his word. The sniper remained on the team and the team prospered under the new commitment.

In relating his story, the sniper wanted others to know the power in being willing to say no. He was not going to risk his career, freedom or life by quietly accepting the substandard conditions he had been asked to work in before. Looking at his little girl made him realize there was a reason to stand up for what was right.

It is time to challenge the status quo and speak out against the things that are wrong with the system. You, too, must be willing to stand up and fight for what you need to be safe and successful. Normally, change in police work is driven by one of two things—effort or tragedy. We can save lives and careers by making a commitment to making the effort now. Fight the power. Not because someone like me says so. Fight because you are worth it. Fight because other people will be affected by what happens to you. Fight because the outcome matters. Fight the power because it is right.

> "Commitment—To fight when others fold, pursue while others retreat, conquer while others quit, and fight when all else is wrong."   —Unknown

GIVE ME AN "S"

Sometimes, I come across as a bit of a cheerleader, but I don't apologize for it. Being a police sniper requires a unique person, who willingly takes on a job of immense responsibility and very little appreciation. Our job is demanding and dangerous. The public, the media, and the rest of the police community have a distorted perception of our job, and almost unrealistic expectations of our abilities. There is no glamour, and little gratitude, only pressure to perform and a standard of perfection. I'm a cheerleader because I think snipers sometimes need to hear words of encouragement. When fatigue, fear and doubt conspire to seduce them to quit, they need to be reminded why they chose the path they did. In the midst of the sweat, dirt and blood, they want to know they choose wisely.

Long ago, I became a sniper because I wanted to try something more challenging and more rewarding than entry work. I worked to excel as a sniper because I came to recognize how important my job really was. I learned early on how many lives depend on me to do well. Now, many years later, I remain a sniper, dedicated to my art and committed to my team. My mission each callout is to save lives, those of my teammates, my friends, and the public I am sworn to protect. I wouldn't want anything less.

I am the eyes on a crisis site. I am the invisible presence in the distance, seeing all, protecting everyone. I am the voice in your headset, the disembodied source of information. I am the protector of life for the innocent, and the deliverer of sudden death to those who would threaten them. I am the line in the sand.

I am a sniper.

APPENDIX

JOIN THE SNIPER COMMUNITY

Since its inception, Snipercraft has drawn interest from snipers from all over the country. People have seen our mission statement, agreed with our cause, and have asked to "join" Snipercraft. Admittedly, we were never really a membership organization. However, we always added those snipers to our ever-growing mailing list. We understood their desire to want to belong to a group of like-minded individuals, who shared their needs, concerns and dedication.

A year or so later, we heard about the American Special Operations Sniper Association, headquartered in Washington. The founder and president, Kino Davis, contacted me and after comparing notes, we knew our respective organizations shared many parallels, and our goals were the same. A partnership was formed, with Snipercraft and ASOSA sharing information, mailing lists, and members. Both organizations benefited from our symbiotic relationship.

Over the years, Kino's many work-related responsibilities robbed him of his ability to maintain his time commitment to ASOSA. Finally, he made the painful decision to give it up. However, he approached me with a request. Snipercraft was asked to step in and fill the void, continuing to offer professional snipers a place to belong. After many long and intense discussions with a circle of my most trusted friends, people with a history of helping the sniper community, it was decided to honor Kino's request. We agreed to embark on a unique project, aimed at furthering our mission to unify the professional sniper community.

The American Sniper Association is a nonprofit organization, meant to identify and address the needs of the sniper community. Our mission is to enhance the image, abilities, proficiency and safety of the professional tactical sniper through education, support and information sharing.

In furtherance of that mission, ASA provides a secure community for special operations snipers to join. It provides a closed network for collecting and disseminating sensitive, operational information. This Association serves as a resource to law enforcement agencies and interested military units in providing facts, figures, tactics, and training information relating to tactical snipers. Snipercraft and ASA continue to publish a quarterly newsletter to provide a venue for sharing information within the sniper community.

Though the Association does not directly provide training, it does sponsor, endorse and promote courses and events that it feels are of the highest quality and are presented by reputable organizations with objectives compatible with the Association's.

The American Sniper Association provides a collective voice for the sniper community, enabling us to address administrators, manufacturers, and trainers as a unified body. There is strength in numbers. When the sniper community speaks as one, the tactical world, and those hoping to garner our favor, will listen to us.

In addition to general membership, we have a number of qualified and ambitious members who serve on our Advisory Board. Board members act as the Association brain trust. They are tasked with a number of grand-scale projects to help us gather information, which will benefit the sniper community. Although ASA is an American-based organization, the Association is open to international membership, provided membership criteria are met.

Membership in the Association is open to active law enforcement, corrections and military personnel only. This policy was adopted after long discussions and is felt to best meet the needs of the organization. Annual dues are $20. Members receive a certificate, a membership card and the quarterly newsletter. They will also become eligible for discounts on registration fees to sniper schools and seminars endorsed by ASA.

As we grow, updated information about the Association will be made available through the newsletter, our friends in the sniper community, like Crosshairs, Inc., SIG Arms Academy, and Snipersonline, and on the web. Look for us at www.americansniper.org. You can e-mail us at info@americansniper.org.

Please sign up and join us. The success of this organization depends on your willingness to be involved and work for the common good. We want every sniper in the world to know about us and belong to this group. Join today, and tell every sniper you know to join. Encourage supervisors to join as well. Through this Association, we hope to educate them and help them to "see through snipers eyes." This can only make your job easier and safer.

Snipercraft continues to provide training, support and two annual events—SniperWeek in Central Florida and the Pacific Conference and Challenge in San Diego, California. Our mission remains the same. We're just growing bigger, stronger, and louder. ASA is part of that growth. And now, you can really "Join the Sniper Community."

ASA SNIPER CERTIFICATION PROGRAM

The position of the police sniper is one of the most important and most difficult in law enforcement. It encompasses high expectations, high liability, and immense individual responsibility. Such a position should require the very highest in standards for selection, training and utilization. Unfortunately, this is not the case.

National standards for police snipers do not exist. What constitutes a sniper varies greatly from jurisdiction to jurisdiction. This variance leads to an inconsistency in selection processes, training of personnel, equipment, policies and most importantly, performance. In this day and age of accountability, this is no longer acceptable.

The American Sniper Association has established a comprehensive process designed to set consistent standards between sniper programs and test standards of performance for individual snipers. It will allow us to recognize professional capability in a uniform manner.

What are the benefits of sniper certification to individual snipers and their agencies? Certification builds trust. It demonstrates a commitment to have a professional sniper program in place to protect the lives of citizens and other law enforcement personnel. It provides a benchmark for programs to achieve and maintain. It will provide a stronger defense against lawsuits brought against your snipers in the performance of their duties. It will provide greater accountability within the agency, as team leaders and administrators have clearly defined standards to expect and enforce. It will tell everyone—the agency, administrators, the media, the courts, and the general public—that your sniper program is well-organized, well-trained, properly-equipped, and recognized by their peers as being fully capable of doing their job in a consistent and professional manner. Who among you would want to put anything less on the streets?

Your agency can apply for ASA Sniper Certification for your individual snipers by following these steps:

1. Send a formal request to the American Sniper Association, asking for the Sniper Certification Program Packet. The request must be on department letterhead, and signed by the agency representative who will be administering the tests. The packet will be mailed to the administrator and must remain in his control throughout the testing process.

2. The request letter should be accompanied by a check or money order for the application fee. This fee helps cover the cost incurred by ASA for this testing and certification process, and is non-refundable. This cost includes postage, printing, supplies, and records maintenance. The fee schedule per agency is as follows: 1 – 4 snipers from one agency, $50; 4 – 8 snipers from one agency, $100; and 8 – 12 snipers from one agency, $125.

3. The request is to be mailed to: American Sniper Association, 472 Lakeside Circle, Fort Lauderdale, FL 33326-4103.

4. No telephone or electronic requests will be accepted.

Be advised, this is not a simple certificate mill. In order to receive certification, your agency will be held to a high, but attainable, standard. Your snipers will have to demonstrate a reasonable level of technical proficiency and knowledge. Your agency will have to provide documentation of a comprehensive sniper program, which is an integral part of a special operations team structure. These standards were not arrived at arbitrarily, but have been established after intensive study of agencies nationwide that have efficient and successful sniper programs. Further input was gained from nationally recognized sniper trainers, administrators and legal experts.

This process is meant to be educational, as well as motivational. It will show you how your sniper program ranks compared to others around the country. It will point out your program's strengths and weaknesses. It will be an accurate gauge of your team's operational readiness. If your snipers or your agency can't meet the standards, hopefully this will serve as an incentive to make the changes necessary to raise the level of your program as soon as possible.

If you think you're ready, apply.

ESTABLISHING A SNIPER TEAM SOP

Part of the Certification Program requirements is having a written SOP covering the sniper element of the agency's tactical team. This is a sample policy to be used as a framework for writing your own. Feel free to customize or modify it as necessary to fit departmental formats.

Standard Operational Procedures: Sniper/Observer

Section 1 - Purpose: To explain the role and responsibilities of the Sniper / Observer

As employed in the police tactical team applications, the role of the Sniper / Observer will be limited to two primary functions:

The Sniper/Observer will use his specialized training, positioning and sight enhancing equipment to observe and report real-time intelligence to his teammates and on-scene command personnel. Since the Sniper / Observer plays such an integral role in intelligence gathering and team protection, he will be deployed as a part of all tactical operations.

The Sniper/Observer will provide protective overwatch to his team, other officers, civilians and / or hostages by bringing precision fire against designated human targets, with the intent to immediately terminate the dangerous actions of that designated target. In this action, state statutes relating to the use of deadly force by police officers, as well as any and all applicable departmental policies will regulate the sniper's decision.

Section 2 - Purpose: To explain Rules of Engagement as applied to the Sniper / Observer

The Sniper / Observer will be authorized to use deadly force against an individual in the following circumstances:

1. To defend himself, another police officer, hostage, or other civilian personnel from the imminent threat of death or great bodily harm.

2. As part of an organized assault by tactical team elements. In this event, the Sniper / Observer would use deadly force against designated targets or targets of opportunity, as the situation or assault plan dictates. These targets would be prioritized and engaged based on the danger they pose to other team members, hostages or civilian personnel. This use of deadly force can be based on collective knowledge, as passed on from other team members or command staff.

3. To prevent the escape from a tactical situation's containment perimeter, if the sniper feels the subject would pose a greater danger of death or great bodily harm to the general public if allowed to continue his actions or succeed in his escape.

Utilization of these Rules of Engagement is subject to meeting or exceeding the standards for use of deadly force as delineated by state statute and departmental policy.

Section 3 - Purpose: To list training requirements for the Sniper/Observer

1. After selection to his position as Sniper / Observer, the candidate will attend and graduate from at least one formal police sniper school, prior to being placed on operational status.

2. To meet the needs of his position, the Sniper / Observer must receive instruction and practice in the following skills and disciplines:

    A. Fieldcraft skills. This is to include, but not limited to, stalking, movement, camouflage, range estimation, and hide selection, construction and management.

    B. Tactics. This is to include, but not limited to, target selection, communications, site diagramming and operation planning.

    C. Marksmanship. Along with a regular, standardized qualification course, this will include practice in cold shot accuracy, multiple targets, moving targets, partially obscured targets, intermediate barriers, up and down hill shooting, various distances and shooting positions, low-light and no light shooting, and decision making.

3. Training will be continued on a regular basis, not less than 8 hours per month.

4. Sniper / Observers will attend formal sniper training every two years at a minimum to upgrade skills and knowledge.

All training planned and done by the Sniper / Observer will be documented in writing. The Sniper Team Leader will maintain records of that training. The Sniper / Observer will maintain individual shooting records, in the form of Shooting Data Books.

Section 4 - Purpose: To list selection criteria and process for the Sniper / Observer

1. Sniper / Observer candidates will be selected from the roster of SWAT team members, based on the listed criteria:

    A. Current team member in good standing
    B. Volunteer for position
    C. Good physical condition
    D. Emotionally mature and stable
    E. Above satisfactory performance ratings

2. After preliminary selection, candidate will submit to the following screening steps:

    A. Oral interview conducted by team selection board
    B. Review of personnel folder
    C. Approval of sniper team members

3. Selected candidate will join sniper team in a probationary status. Regular status will be achieved after the candidate has graduated from a formal police sniper school and has passed the department sniper qualification course.

Section 5 - Purpose: To list qualification and performance standards for the Sniper / Observer

To achieve and maintain operational status as a Sniper / Observer, each sniper team member will be required to meet the following standards:

1. Each Sniper / Observer will attend and graduate a formal police sniper school.

2. Each Sniper / Observer will pass the team qualification course. The course will be designed to test the Sniper / Observer's skills as they apply to realistic job-related applications. This may include cold shots, partially exposed targets, stress shots, moving targets, and intermediate barriers. This course will be administered at least four times a year. Each course will require a score of 90% or better to pass.

3. Failure to pass two consecutive qualification courses will result in removal of the Sniper / Observer from operational status until he is able to demonstrate proficiency with two consecutive passing scores.

SNIPER UTILIZATION SURVEY

What is the average distance of a police sniper shooting in the United States? When most people in the tactical community are asked this question, the answers tend to be in the range of 70 – 77 yards. When asked about the source of their information, almost all allude to "the FBI statistics."

Would it come as a shock to you to hear this is a myth?

Last year, the American Sniper Association tried to obtain a copy of that report to study and evaluate. We checked a variety of resources and followed referrals to people who would have the report. Much to our surprise, we discovered the report does not exist. According to the FBI, they do not, nor have they ever, collected that kind of data.

For as long as I can remember, that "70 something" number has been reported as fact. Schools, manuals and articles refer to it to this very day. It has been used as the justification for training, equipping and deploying snipers for decades. The foundation for all of those beliefs and practices does not exist.

Knowing the importance of this information, and the training and deployment issues it will raise, ASA decided to embark on a major project. We currently have a team of volunteers contacting every law enforcement agency in America to find out if they have a sniper element. If so, then we have a series of questions about any shootings in which their team may have been involved. From the questions asked in the survey, we are learning from what distances shots are being taken. We are learning about times, conditions, weapons, scopes and ammunition used, shot placement, results and bullet performance. We are also collecting anecdotal information from individual sniper incidents, each of which has important lessons learned. And for the first time in history, all of this information will exist in one formal report. This will be a monumental accomplishment.

The finished report will not be a dry recitation of statistics. It will contain facts and numbers, but will include lessons learned and details of specific incidents.

- In addition to being able to finally establish the real "average distance" of a police sniper engagement, we will also point out the longest and shortest engagements. There are special circumstances surrounding both, with important learning points.
- Readers will learn the times of day and night shootings have occurred. This will emphasize the importance of varying training hours.
- The report will also present evidence to support the need to practice shooting positions beyond prone bipod. Snipers have had to employ a variety of improvised positions to accomplish their missions.
- Anecdotal evidence will also be presented showing the high percentage of sniper shootings that result in through and through wounds. Collateral damage is a legitimate concern for snipers as a result.

Perhaps you are wondering why any of this matters. What will be the impact and importance of this information? Based on what we have discovered so far, we believe:

- Rifle manufacturers will find out how their products are really working in the field. From actual operational information gathered from teams, they will be made aware of successes, as well as the failures some weapon systems have suffered.
- Ammunition manufacturers will see statistical data and empirical proof of the over penetration problems match grade ammunition continues to have. Hopefully, this will lead to changes in bullet designs before a tragedy occurs.
- Night vision manufacturers will be able to learn how and when their equipment is needed and is being used. They may also learn why it is not being used by some agencies.
- Designers and producers of auxiliary tactical gear will learn what role their equipment may play in sniper operations, and what needs to be changed or improved.
- SWAT commanders, trainers and administrators will know with

certainty the historical distances, circumstances and outcomes of sniper incidents from around the country. This information will directly affect training, policies, budgeting priorities, equipment purchases and deployments far into the future.

While this is obviously a worthy and important cause, we are surprised at the difficulties we have faced so far in completing the process. In fact, the process has been as much a learning experience as the finished product will be. To our amazement, some agencies have kept such poor records, they can't provide accurate information, and have offered estimates based on individual recollections.

We have called some agencies repeatedly, only to be passed from person to person, trying to find someone to answer the survey questions. Sometimes this is because the person with the answers isn't readily available. Other times we are aware of a conscious run around. Although the survey finally gets done, it makes the process very labor intensive.

A number of agencies have balked at cooperating with the survey at all. There is still a reluctance to openly share information with outside agencies. We must expend a fair amount of time and energy convincing administrators this project will benefit them and the rest of the tactical community. In one contact, a police chief told us point blank he would not release information to us under any circumstances. He would not offer an explanation why. The "Code of Silence" in law enforcement continues to exist and hamper progress. We are not seeking to critique any of the shootings we research. We are gathering data for statistical and historical purposes only. The actions of that agency speak for themselves, without any public comment from ASA.

The content of the report will not specifically identify any officer or agency. The information we collect is regarded as confidential and will not be made available to the general public. The finished publication will be circulated within the community, mailed only to officers and administrators at their agency.

By the time you are reading this, the data initial collection portion of the project has been finally completed. Now, the next phase will require organizing, collating, publishing and distributing the final report. We want to be able to print and distribute the final report to participating agencies free of charge. We also plan to maintain accurate updates of the collected data for several years into the future to keep our data current. In order to facilitate this, we are asking every agency to voluntarily submit a copy of the survey form any time their snipers use deadly force. A copy of the form is available at the ASA website.

If you have questions about the survey, or would like to add a report, please contact ASA at info@americansniper.org, or call Richard Morey, 863-784-7285.

Completion of the survey and publication of the report will be announced in the American Sniper Association's newsletter, on our website, www.americansniper.org, and by direct mail to the agencies that participate in the process. To make sure you are notified, join ASA and contribute to the survey.

RECOMMENDED READING

I consider these essential additions to the library of every sniper serious about his art. They represent a wide range of sniper issues and concerns.

After the Echo; A Survival Guide For Police & Military Snipers,
Russ Clagett

Heads or Tails: A True Hostage Story of Terror, Torture and Ultimate Survival, Lisa Monique Joseph

On Killing, Lt. Col. Dave Grossman

On Combat, Lt. Col. Dave Grossman & Loren Christensen

Deadly Force Encounters, Dr. Alexis Artwohl & Loren Christensen

Officer Involved Shootings and Use of Force, Practical Investigative Techniques, David E. Hatch

Snipercraft: The Art of the Police Sniper, Derrick D. Bartlett

A Terrible Thunder, Peter Hernon

A Sniper in the Tower, Gary Lavergne

Sniper, Mark Spicer

Sniper, Peter Brookesmith

Sniper and Stalk & Kill, Adrian Gilbert

One Day in September, Simon Reeve

The Management of Police Specialized Tactical Units,
Tomas C. Mijares, Ronald McCarthy and David B. Perkins

Police Rifles, Richard Fairburn